EXPLORING THE BIBLE

George Otto Simms

Exploring
the Bible

THE COLUMBA PRESS • A P C K

First published in 1996 by
THE COLUMBA PRESS
55A Spruce Avenue, Stillorgan Industrial Park,
Blackrock, Co Dublin
and
APCK
St Ann's Bookcentre, Dawson Street, Dublin 2

Cover by Bill Bolger
Origination by The Columba Press
Printed in Ireland by Colour Books Ltd, Dublin

ISBN 1 85607 150 2

Acknowledgements
The publishers gratefully acknowledge the assistance of Dr
David Egar and Professor John Bartlett in the final preparation
of this book for the press.

Contents

CHAPTER 1

One volume: many books

It is hoped that some of the description and discussion in this book will serve as an introduction to a study and enjoyment of the Bible.

No book about the Bible can convey the atmosphere and the grandeur of these scriptures. A summary of the Bible's contents and an outline of its characters cannot serve as a substitute for the reading of the Book itself. This attempted summary of the Old and New Testaments can only claim to be a temporary companion for those encouraged to read further.

The word 'Bible' means either 'book' or 'books'. It is called holy because it is a collection of writings about God and his relationship with people.

A great variety of literature is included within the covers of the single volume, commonly printed and published today in many versions and translations. In addition to history and chronicle the 'scriptures' contain law, prophecy, poetry, liturgy, personal letters, proverbs and wise sayings about faith and life. In spite of this variety, there is a common theme – the ways of God with his people.

The Bible as Revelation

The Bible consists of two 'Testaments'. The word 'testament' indicates the relationship between God and people. This is also called a covenant-relationship which states how things are between one person and another. The Old Testament and the New Testament reveal the relationship of the world with God. Thus the Bible belongs to a people, a covenanted people, a community loved and held together by God. The Old Testament is the Jewish people's book. The Old Testament and the New Testament, when combined, form the scriptures of the Christian Church.

'revelation' is often applied in general terms to these
~y were chosen to bear witness to the meaning of the
_ch surrounded the writing of them. They were counted
as documents which expressed with a special authority what
was the will and instruction of God in the history of his people.

Revelation, in the somewhat daring definition of Archbishop
William Temple, 'consists in the coincidence of event and interpretation'. The personalities of the Bible in their actions and re-
actions demonstrate God's dealings with those whom he created
and continued to care for. Many today are aware that they live
within the drama of the Bible. They find in the study of its background and heritage much that is of vital importance for the better understanding of themselves.

Two Testaments

The story of Israel is told in the Old Testament. It is a history,
first and foremost, of the faith of a people. It has been called by
some a 'salvation history', for it traces the chequered fortunes of
those who belonged to God and had a calling from God to do his
will and obey his laws. At first the people of the Old Testament
were wanderers; then they settled in the country later to be
called Palestine, a promised land, where they had roots; exile and
captivity followed the conquest of that land by strong military
forces; destruction and distress figure frequently in the story. It
is a history of God's judgment as well as God's care and love.
Often the faith of the nation is kept alive by the obedience and
loyal response of the few. At other times, disobedience to God's
law heralds disaster. Yet there were survivors. The influence of
'the remnant' was strong because their allegiance to God did not
falter.

The Hebrew Bible printed today, with vowel pointing and accents, is known as the 'Massoretic' text. The name probably
indicates 'traditional', and comes from an authoritative edition
of the Hebrew text produced by Jewish scholars as late as the
sixth to eighth centuries A.D.

There were earlier written Hebrew texts. The discovery in the
1940s of the 'Dead Sea Scrolls' at Qumran has, for example,
brought to light a text of Isaiah, dating from 200 B.C., without
the addition of vowel-points or accents. This is possibly the earliest known manuscript of the Old Testament surviving. It is

also remarkable that the differences between the Qumran text and the Massoretic, though important, are not so numerous as might at first have been supposed.

Behind the writing of the Old Testament there was a long period of oral tradition. The incidents and the teaching were passed on from generation to generation by word of mouth, by a people whose family life was strong. The strength of the religion they learned and taught was made more persistent in a land where surrounding nations and tribes, great and small, followed other religions and ways of worship which conflicted with the beliefs of the Jews, and were often abhorrent to them.

Aramaic is also used in parts of the Old Testament (Ezra 4:5-6; 8:7, 12-26; Jer 10:11 and Dan 2:4-7:28). This language, called after the region of Aram in northern Palestine and Syria, was used from the tenth century B.C. onwards. By the time of Christ, it was the most widely spoken language in Palestine, while Hebrew was used for literary and liturgical purposes. Aramaic and Hebrew are closely related.

The New Testament extends the story of a people whose roots were in Israel but were now no longer tied to any particular country or race. The Christians saw themselves bound together in a new covenant. Their life 'in Christ', as it was called, had a new status. All could find a unity and a solidarity through Christ in the power of the Holy Spirit; Jew and Greek, slave and free, male and female discovered a new unity in their Christian life.

Although Jesus and the earliest Christians probably spoke Aramaic, the New Testament was written in Greek. It was Greek which was the common language of most of the civilised world at the time, and as Christianity spread, Greek rapidly became the language of most Christians.

The earliest known New Testament manuscript is a fragment of papyrus containing part of the passion narrative from the gospel according to John. It may date from as early as A.D. 130 – only decades after the gospel was written – and is kept in the John Rylands Library in Manchester. Two of the most important New Testament manuscripts are housed together in the Chester Beatty Library in Dublin. These are the oldest surviving copies

of the four gospels and the Acts of the Apostles contained together in one book, and the oldest surviving copy of the letters
of Paul, also in one papyrus book. Both of these treasured texts
date from about A.D. 200.

The Canon

At the end of the first century of the Christian era (around A.D.
100), the Jewish rabbis authorised 'the Law, the Prophets and
the Writings'. These Jewish scriptures, called the Old Testament
by Christians, were compiled over a long period of several hundred years before the authorised list of books, called the 'Canon',
was drawn up. The earliest books to be accorded special authority, giving definitive expression to the relationship between God
and humankind, were probably the five books of the Pentateuch.

The books of the prophets later also received recognition as authoritative. As the people saw their history as a unique witness
to their relationship with God, they termed the historical books of
Joshua, Judges, I and II Samuel and I and II Kings as 'the earlier
prophets', alongside 'the later prophets', the great figures of
Isaiah, Jeremiah, Ezekiel, and the twelve minor prophets. The
'Writings' were the last books of the Old Testament to be given
special recognition as authoritative, or canonical. They included
the Psalms, the Proverbs, and Ecclesiastes, as well as the dramatic
stories of Job, Esther and Ruth.

By the third century B.C., the Jewish community had spread
outside its traditional homeland. There were large Jewish communities outside of Palestine, who often no longer fluently
spoke the Hebrew language in which their scriptures were written. As a result, the Jewish scriptures were gradually translated.
The translation made into Greek in the Egyptian city of
Alexandria was particularly important. Legend tells how the
translation of the Law was commissioned by the Egyptian ruler
Ptolemy, and was prepared by seventy scholars working from
copies supplied by the High Priest in Jerusalem. From this legend, which is usually seen as unhistorical, comes the name
'Septuagint' (from the Latin for seventy) for the Greek translation of the Jewish scriptures.

In time, other writings, which had been composed in Greek or had become popular in that language, came to be seen as authoritative by Greek-speaking Jews. These included books like the Wisdom of Solomon, Ecclesiasticus, and the books of the Maccabees. When the Hebrew canon of authoritative sacred scripture was drawn up these books were not included.

The Greek translation of the Jewish scriptures was the Bible of the early Christians. Alongside the Septuagint, some early Christian writings also took on definitive significance for them. By the fourth century, an authoritative canon of early Christian writings was agreed. This became the Christian New Testament, while the Septuagint became the Christian Old Testament.

At the time of the Reformation in the sixteenth century, the reformers treated the original Hebrew text, rather than the Latin Vulgate, as their basic text for the Old Testament. They also adopted the Hebrew Old Testament canon. As a result, books which were contained in the Septuagint canon, but which had been excluded by the rabbis from the Hebrew canon, were also excluded from the Protestant canon of the Old Testament. These books were considered edifying reading, but were not held to be sacred scripture in a definitive sense. They became known as the 'Apocrypha', or the 'hidden' books.

Unity in Diversity

Christians find in the phrase 'the church to teach, the Bible to prove' a guiding line to illustrate the connection between the church and the scriptures. The Christian Church existed before the New Testament was compiled and declared to be an authentic witness of Christian life and faith; the covenant, or God's promise to his people, was proclaimed long before the birth of Jesus Christ. The Christians see in the Old Testament promises which were later interpreted and fulfilled.

Christians in their worship sing Psalms from the Old Testament. In their liturgy, readings are chosen from both Old and New Testaments. These traditions emphasise the unity of the Bible. The close connections between the people of Israel and the Christian people were made clear when the references in the New Testament writings to 'the scriptures', made by Jesus and others, always recalled 'the Law, the Prophets, and the Writings', later to be known as the Old Testament.

Thus the Christians hold that, in spite of the differences between the two testaments, 'the Old Testament is not contrary to the New'. A famous comment clarifies this: 'The Old Testament is made plain in the New, and the New Testament lies hidden in the Old.' What is promised in the Old is fulfilled in the New. The Old Testament is revealed (Latin: *patet*) in the New; the New is concealed (*latet*) in the Old.

This connection was emphasised constantly because, on more than one occasion in the history of the Christian Church, attempts have been made to exclude the use of the Old Testament from public worship and to ignore its teaching. Clearly, however, Jesus himself expounded the Old Testament scriptures in his teaching, sometimes throwing new light upon their meaning, at other times upholding their message, transcending and renewing the traditions into which he himself had been born. Significant Christian words, such as *kingdom, redemption,* and *justification,* cannot be fully understood apart from their Old Testament context and background. Just as in the understanding of current affairs today the past often throws light on the problems of the present, so the 'new teaching' given by Jesus is appreciated more fully when the religious beliefs and presuppositions which coloured the minds of his hearers are examined. The environment and the culture of the nation to which Jesus belonged in his life on earth become important subjects of study if the words of the scripture are to be properly understood.

Critical Study of the Bible

From as early as the year A.D. 200 books have been written about the Bible, with a view to explaining its message and interpreting its teaching.

There is nothing new or strange about an approach to the scriptures which involves a critical study of the background and authorship of its several books. A scholarly examination of the written words has been made ever since translations in different languages have been undertaken. Criticism has a positive quality and, in a broad sense, includes comment, interpretation, evaluation, and analysis of the language used to express religious thinking. Such an activity need not be destructive. When carried out with the support of sound evidence and honest assessment, such judgements help the reader to understand the intention of the writer and the meaning of what has been written.

For a long time, biblical scholars have appreciated that the scriptures are not purely historical documents. On the other hand, the religious truths and experiences which they record are often expressed in a particular historical setting. It has been found important, therefore, to search for the dating of what has been written, to observe the significance of the religious language used at each period and to take account of the varieties in literary style, of the poetry of the scriptures as well as of the prose. It has been pointed out that the books of the Bible present not a 'still', but a moving picture.

In particular, the manner in which God himself is referred to in the narrative signifies a gradual development in theological thinking. The different names for the deity and the various adjectives describing the character and activity of God enable us to appreciate a gradual unfolding of much that still remains mysterious. There is in the written text a progressive revelation of timeless, spiritual truths perceived through events in history and in many different kinds of human experience. The Bible starts with God, not with any argument about his existence. Affirmations, rather than philosophical proofs, are found in the scriptures.

Fresh light is constantly thrown upon the text by recent discoveries and archaeological excavations. Such evidence as has been provided by the Qumran documents (Dead Sea Scrolls) since the late 1940s provides an example of this. Archaeological expeditions in the Middle East continue to help with the task of dating and interpreting the scriptures, often more clearly understood when seen as community documents, the product of much that has been handed on by word of mouth before being committed to writing.

Work continues on the actual text of each book. This so-called 'lower criticism' involves the detailed study of manuscripts. Some of these have been well-known for many centuries. Their text has been checked and corrected when further evidence has emerged, for example, from Egyptian papyri and Qumran scrolls during this twentieth century.

The 'higher critics' supply, with what evidence is available, up-to-date information about the authorship of the books, the date of the writing or the editing or the compilation of the texts. The word 'redaction' is often applied to the work of a reviser, who may have undertaken, for example, the rearrangement of a narrative, told twice-over when derived from more than one source. There is more than one account of the Creation, the Flood, and much else in the Bible. Accordingly, a study of sources, and of collections of writings and sayings becomes a significant, as well as a fascinating, pursuit for the biblical student.

Much help is also given to the reader of the Bible by the summaries provided in various translations. In the Authorised Version of A.D. 1611 (The King James Bible) the headings, in italics, at the top of each column on the printed page point to the subject dealt with below. These 'running titles' are much older than the translation and are based on the Latin summaries (*breves causae*) found in many versions of Jerome's Vulgate text of the Bible (dating from A.D. 383). In recent English translations, the paragraphs with appropriate headings and titles facilitate the reading and the study of the scriptures, and encourage ways of meditating upon short sections and particular incidents. The New International Version (1978), for example, prints the words in such a way as to distinguish poetry from prose and includes clear cross-headings. The chapter-numbers, introduced by Stephen Langton in the thirteenth century, are still used for reference. So also are the verse-numbers, of a later date, introduced in the sixteenth century and associated with the name of Stephanus (Etienne), the biblical critic and scholar.

Commentaries written about the books of the Bible are many in number. These aids to Bible-reading and many others, including maps of Palestine and the Mediterranean to match different stages in history, will assist the general reader. A chronological table, outlining historical events referred to in the biblical narrative, will increase an understanding of the prophecies, psalms, gospels and letters within the Bible. They will also be reminders that the scriptures, written by believers for believers, were also rooted in the world and formed a woven pattern, as has been remarked, of both 'history and interpretation'.

Versions and Translations

The earliest translation of the Bible was the Greek version of the Hebrew scriptures made for the use of Greek-speaking Jews in Egypt, known as the Septuagint (LXX). There are some significant differences between the Hebrew and Greek versions. The order of the books is different, and some apocryphal writings are included in the Greek version. It seems likely, at least, that the Pentateuch was translated into Greek in Egypt before the middle of the third century B.C. The Jews in Alexandria at the time were more familiar with Greek than with Hebrew or Aramaic. The style is Alexandrian as we learn from the vernacular of the papyri. The author of the preface to Ecclesiasticus leads us to conclude that by 132 B.C. the translation of the Old Testament as we know it was complete. The Old Testament quotations in the New Testament usually follow the text of the Septuagint.

A need for a Latin version of the Bible was first felt among Christians in North Africa. In Rome itself the language of the Christians continued to be Greek until after A.D. 150. So the first Latin translations, called Old Latin, were made from the LXX in the case of the Old Testament, and the original Greek of the New Testament. This version was revised from the year A.D. 382 by Jerome at the request of Pope Damasus. Jerome later went to Bethlehem and, on the way, at Caesarea, he made a second revision of the Psalter from Origen's text. This version was known as the Gallican Psalter, much used afterwards in Gaul and the West. From it Coverdale made his version in English (1535). This is now printed in the Book of Common Prayer. Realising that Hebrew was the original Old Testament language, Jerome made a fresh translation, which became known as the Vulgate (the common or standard version). This was an important undertaking and indicated the character of the Hebrew text in the fourth century, several hundred years before the Massoretic text.

By A.D. 600, the gospels as well as some other books had been translated into Latin, Syriac, Coptic, Gothic, Armenian, Georgian, Ethiopic, Nubian, and Sogdian (Iran). For all except Latin and Sogdian, the translation was the first written literature.

The Latin version of the scriptures became the principal form of the Bible used in western Christianity for many centuries. In the fourteenth century, John Wycliffe made a translation into English from the Latin Vulgate. His translation was opposed by the authorities of his day, and did not become widely known. The introduction of printing by Gutenberg in 1456 meant that

many copies of a book like the Bible could be produced easily
and cheaply. Shortly afterwards, the theologians of the
Reformation stressed the supreme authority of the Bible for
Christian doctrine and faith. They endeavoured to provide
translations of the scriptures in the languages of the ordinary
people. The ease of production brought about by printing
helped greatly in making their translations widely available.

Martin Luther's first German translation of the New Testament
was published in 1522, based on the Greek text published in
1519 by the classical scholar Erasmus of Rotterdam. In 1526,
William Tyndale, living in exile in Germany, published his
English translation of the New Testament. His translation of the
Pentateuch was published in 1530. Tyndale reproduced the con-
sonants of the divine name 'YHWH' with the vowels of
'aDoNaY' ('my Lord', substituted for YHWH when the Hebrew
text was read aloud) to coin the name Jehovah. Miles Coverdale
published his first translation of the Bible in 1535, and also produced the revision known as the 'Great Bible' of 1539.

The 'Authorised' Version of 1611, although probably never in
fact officially authorised, was produced by fifty-four theologians, working in Oxford, Cambridge and Westminster. They
based their work on the Bishops' Bible (1568), and consulted earlier translations like the Geneva Bible (1560) and the versions of
Tyndale and Coverdale. This version became known as the King
James Version, and received widespread recognition throughout the whole of the English-speaking world.

With the discovery of older and more reliable manuscripts, especially of the Greek New Testament, a need was felt for new
translations by the end of the last century. The Revised Version
was published in 1881, followed by the Revised Standard
Version in 1952. In recent decades, many more new translations
have been produced, continuing the attempt to render the scriptures accurately into the everyday language of the people. These
include the *New English Bible* (1961 and 1970), the *Jerusalem Bible*
(1966 and 1985), the *New International Version* (1978), and the
New Revised Standard Version (1989).

PART I

The Old Testament

CHAPTER 2

Introduction

The Old Testament begins the story of God's relationship with the world. It moves forwards from the start of that relationship in creation to depict Israel's calling as a people special to God. Faithfulness and failure are interwoven throughout the story of the people's experiences. The justice and righteousness which are characteristic of God's commitment to the covenant with his people remain constant both in times of judgement and of joy.

God was seen at work in many differing and often in mysterious ways either through individuals or through groups of people. Each book of the Old Testament in a distinctive way reveals something about the mind and will of the Maker.

The first five books of the Old Testament, called the *Pentateuch*, emphasise in different ways the divine ordering of life upon earth, and especially of life in the community which has been chosen to make known God's will in his creation.

Genesis does not attempt to give the kind of account of the origins of creation such as might be expected from biologists or geologists; its first two chapters provide two interpretations of the thinking mind and deliberate will behind creation. Later sections of Genesis illustrate the disorders of the world in a period before historical events were chronicled. The Flood, for instance, tells of God's judgement; the tower of Babel is a reminder of the disastrous consequences of human pride and the ignoring of God.

Exodus presents in historical form the providential deliverance of God's faithful community from the darkness and slavery of Egypt, commonly dated to the thirteenth century B.C. With the leadership of Moses, the journey was made across the Red Sea ('the sea of reeds') through 'the great and terrible wilderness' towards a promised land, where the people could have freedom to practise their faith. This deliverance was never forgotten and is constantly referred to throughout the whole Bible. The events not only made history but also assured succeeding generations that God rescued his people and gave them a place of their own in the world. God also tested and disciplined them; through Moses, the Ten Commandments laid a lasting foundation of morality to inspire a love of God and a love of neighbour in a life of spiritual worship and practical service.

The details and the requirements of the laws and ceremonies which brought unity and a sense of destiny to the chosen people are set out in the books of Leviticus, Numbers, and Deuteronomy.

The meaning and interpretation of the events in the nation's history are seen as part of the prophecy which continued to reveal 'in many and various ways' God's communication and relationship with his people, even when they fail to respond to his will and his way of life.

The prophets articulated God's will for his people in the midst of their daily lives and the history of their nation. At times their message was one of judgement and reproof. At other times, they spoke words of comfort and hope. Above all, they interpreted the life of the people from the standpoint of the people's relationship with God.

Amos, the earliest of the writing prophets, introduces his message with a confident directness. His 'thus saith the Lord' lends authority to his statements and reveals that what was taking place in the public and private life of the day was subject to the rule of God and must be judged by divine standards.

Hosea, in his prophecy, pointed to God's mercy and love in the midst of trouble. Isaiah promised that a small remnant of the chosen people would return from their captivity at the hands of their enemies and thus be able to keep their faith alive. This more politically minded prophet revealed how God works through minorities. A fuller examination of the later chapters of Isaiah will be made at a later stage. Jeremiah writes of the urgency for a new covenant; his words encouraged a new approach to the laws of God when he wrote: 'I will put my law, saith the Lord, in their inward parts, and in their hearts I will write it.' Ezekiel, out of the loneliness of an exile far from the homeland, promises the restoration of temple worship through which the people will find once more a spiritual centre for their life as a nation.

The last of the Old Testament prophetic books to be written contains a vision of what would come in the future. It is a striking fact that the latest of the prophets, Daniel, expressed his message in apocalyptic language not unlike the imagery of the vision of John 'the Divine' in the final book of the Bible. Apocalypse, or 'the uncovering of what was hidden' in Daniel's visions, was coloured by the grim experiences during the tyrannical reign of Antiochus Epiphanes about the year 170 B.C. In spite of this tale of destruction and despair, there is a promise and a prophecy of a 'Son of Man'. Someone is expected to come to the rescue. 'Blessed is he that waiteth' (Dan 12:2) is the positive message at the end of the book.

The psalms, the proverbs, and the books of Job, Ecclesiastes, and the Song of Songs are among the books known as 'the Writings' in the Hebrew Bible. Many of psalms may well have been used in the liturgies of the temple in Jerusalem. They include great songs of praise and celebration, as well as cries of deep anguish and prayers for help and protection.

The book of Job unfolds a drama revolving around the tragedy and mystery of human suffering. It reflects on the justice of God, and shows the vindication of one who trusted in God's justification. In several of the other 'writings', the theme of 'wisdom' is important. Through the meditation and study of wisdom in these books, a deeper understanding of the mystery and righteousness of God can be gained.

Dating the books of the Old Testament

It is not possible to assign exact dates to the final form in which the books of the Old Testament were written. The conclusions which many scholars have reached with approximate dating are listed here:

Century B.C.

VIII	Amos, Hosea, Micah, Isaiah (chapters 1-39)
VII	Deuteronomy, Jeremiah, Zephaniah, Habakkuk, Nahum

VI   Jeremiah, Lamentations, Ezekiel, Isaiah (chapters
            40-66), Haggai, Obadiah, Zechariah, Judges,
            Ruth, I and II Samuel, I and II Kings

V   Malachi, Joel, Song of Songs

IV   Genesis, Exodus, Leviticus, Numbers, Joshua
            (written down from earlier sources)

III   I and II Chronicles, Ezra, Nehemiah, Job,
            Ecclesiastes, Jonah

II   Psalms (in the completed collection), Proverbs,
            Esther, Daniel

However much the dating of the books of the Old Testament may
vary among scholars, it is clear that the traditional order in which
the books were printed and published reflects the subject matter
rather than the chronology of the final form of the text when edited. The story of the people of God told from the beginning was
compiled in many different ways. Sources both oral and written
can be traced in its pages. The discoveries of archaeologists, and
the records of secular historical events support some of the conclusions on which the scholars have reached agreement. In addition, the style of the writing, the use of language, and the development of thought in the individual books, have been taken into account and made this chronological table acceptable, although
many uncertainties still remain.

CHAPTER 3

The Pentateuch:

Genesis, Exodus, Leviticus, Numbers, Deuteronomy

The first five books of the Bible, called by the Greek word, Pentateuch (*five books*), contain the Torah. Torah means more than 'law'; this Hebrew word for law also includes 'instruction'. These books, committed to their final written form at a much later period, record collections of narratives and laws, drawn from different groups in various parts of Palestine. For centuries, this teaching had apparently been handed on by word of mouth.

Scholars, in spite of many difficulties in tracing origins, generally agree that some four sources, labelled with the letters J, E, D, and P, lie behind the text of the Pentateuch. J symbolised Judah and the use of the divine name Jahweh (or Yahweh, usually translated 'the Lord'); E for Ephraim and the use of Elohim for God (usually translated 'God'); both of these traditions stem from about the ninth century B.C.; D is for Deuteronomy begun in the northern kingdom and completed in seventh century in Jerusalem; while P is the Priestly document begun in Exile 587-535 B.C. Fifth-century priests are thought to have woven their own and other traditions into a connected document.

In recent years, scholars have also stressed that the Pentateuch is much more than a compilation of sources. The older texts and traditions have been woven together to make up a new unified whole. This whole merits study in its own right, apart from the study of the sources underlying it. Likewise, each of the five books of the Pentateuch comprises a distinct piece of literature, each telling its own story, drawing out particular aspects of the older traditions used in its composition.

Some scholars add Joshua to the Pentateuch and see in the first six books (the so-called Hexateuch) the theme of Yahweh making a covenant with Abraham and again at Sinai which finds fulfilment with the arrival of the people, rescued and chosen, in the promised land. The central subject is not creation, but salvation and election.

The Pentateuch was the first part of the scriptures to be recognised as standard (canonical), authoritative teaching. In fact, this was the only canon of teaching that the Samaritans recognised. The Samaritans became separated from the Jews in the fourth century, at the time when the Torah was finally brought to its complete form.

In Genesis, the different sources can be traced in some sections more easily than in others. It appears that the J writer has a style of simple storytelling with a clear, straight-forward narrative. E is rather more mystical, with references to dreams and the otherworldly presence of angels, while P's style is more technical and deeply concerned with the weightier matters of doctrine and worship.

GENESIS

The creation of the world is recorded from two sources (Gen 1:1-2:3 and Gen 2:4-25). Chapter 1 is shaped in the literary form of a meditation. It does not contain any speculation about the existence of God, but rather affirms his wonderful act of creation. There is both praise and declaration in the opening words: 'In the beginning God created the heavens and the earth' (Gen 1:1). The reader is encouraged to reflect and contemplate. He responds in wonder and worship. The astronaut on the journey back to earth from the moon found that the opening words of Genesis matched his mood and meditation. Those words mark the opening of a preface to the history of the Hebrew people. Genesis, chapters 1-11, deals with the universe, the wide world, the early times of human civilisation. In this cosmic setting, the changes and destiny of the chequered history of the Jews in Palestine will be viewed. Out of all the peoples and nations in human history, the calling and responsibilities of one particular people will be the subject of the Old Testament.

There is a sense in which the creation narratives present teaching not only about God but also about human nature.

Creation is distinct from God. God is not the world, yet the world belongs to him. What is created is good, therefore it has a purpose. Light and darkness are called 'day' and 'night'; these terms indicate order and control. The recurring round with 'evening' and 'morning' provides a framework for living. Those reading and pondering upon the stages of creation are drawn into the drama of it all. There are further contrasts, with 'sea' surrounding 'dry land', life of varying orders emerges, plant and tree life, living creatures, birds, fishes and beasts and finally human life. The human being made in the 'likeness' of the Creator has creative duties to carry out 'on behalf of' God. There is a sense of climax at Gen 1:27:

> So God created man
> In his own image,
> In the image of God
> he created him;
> male and female
> he created them.

The phrases suggest an affirmation of faith in the shape of a creed. The creative poetry of scripture expresses in literary, cultic or devotional form, rather than in the language of physical science, the wonder and the glory of creation. If there are comparatively few references in the rest of the Old Testament to these opening chapters of Genesis, we find the creation theme nevertheless echoed many times in colourful psalms (Ps 104 and 148), also in Job 28 and elsewhere. Careful choice of words reflects spiritual teaching. Some 'priestly' thought-forms influence the word-picture. Is the phrase 'two great lights' influenced by the teaching of astrologers in a Mesopotamian background? It is quite probable that the substitution of 'greater light' for 'sun' and 'lesser light' for 'moon' served as a safe-guard against sun- and moon-worship. There is only one God in the creation narrative of Genesis; even if Babylonian parallels are striking and fascinating, there is no suggestion in Genesis of rivalry among many gods. The one Creator-God is in control of both light and darkness.

Other phrases emphasise the religious and theological interpretation of creation. The very word 'created' rather than simply 'made' points to a relationship between creature and creator which is both close and enduring. The difficult phrase 'image and likeness' (Gen 1:26) is a way of indicating 'the whole man';

and the description 'very good' marks the perfection and complete harmony of 'the glorious work' achieved. Even 'the rest', 'the sabbath' at the climax is a sign, not of God's anthropomorphism, but of his holiness. It is a holy rest (Gen 2:2f).

In the second account of the creation (Gen 2:4-25), man is the centre of attention; so also is his destiny. He has roots on earth. There is a play upon words in the Hebrew (*adam*, man; *adamah*, ground). He has responsibilities in creation. He is not, however, the independent judge of what is good and what is evil. The veto set upon the eating of the tree of knowledge of good and evil makes this point clear (Gen 2:17). Man learns what is good from God; he by himself cannot make this distinction. God decides what is good and what is evil.

Chapter 2 provides teaching through the story it tells. The narrative is more concerned with the earth than with the universe. The sowing, gardening, and the naming of the animals take place in a man's world. Man's close partnership with 'woman' is reflected in the Hebrew words (*ish*, man and *ishah*, woman). Man becomes a living creature only when inspired with 'the breath of life' (Gen 2:7).

Chapter 3 presents in dramatic form man's 'first disobedience and the fruit'. The temptation 'to be like gods, knowing good and evil' was strong (Gen 3:5). 'Knowing' in Hebrew idiom is more like 'experiencing' rather than 'having intellectual knowledge'. To know, in a sense, means 'to have power', 'to know how', and there is a fatal attraction in the possibility of exercising power beyond the conditions and limits appointed by God in his work of creation. Pride lies at the root of the separation from God and the desire of the man and the woman to be free and independent (Gen 3:6 and 7). The subtle half-truths of the serpent are dangerously deceptive. The consequences of this experience are expressed in terms of fear and shame (Gen 3:7 and 10).

These first three chapters illustrate, in the language of drama and devotion, the meaning of the world and of human life in the light of God's purposes. In the chapters which follow, the consequences of pride and other examples of rebellion against God's will and purpose continue the story. Adam and Eve (the man and the woman) have a role to play in their world, although it is marked by labour and suffering. Work was not a curse; there was work to be done in Paradise (Gen 2:15). God is both good and strict, but his judgement is tempered with mercy. The first question addressed by God to man after the separation was a searching one. The 'Where are you?' (Gen 3:9) introduced the long history of redemption. The recurring theme of God searching for man and man hiding from God reveals the mercy and judgement of the creator. Sometimes, indeed, God seems to be hidden, while man searches with perseverance. Examples of this two-way movement, this spiritual hide-and-seek, are plentiful (Ps 139 and 89; Job 23:3; Ex 3:6).

In the lives of Cain (Gen 4), Lamech and his son Noah (Gen 5 and 6), as well as among peoples such as those in Canaan and Babel (Gen 11), the goodness and severity of God are combined.

In the account of the Flood, with certain parallels in Babylonian tradition, the punishment of the wicked and the salvation of the righteous are evident.

The rainbow, as a sign of God's covenant with Noah, symbolises God's everlasting mercy (Is 54:9). The never-to-be-forgotten bow in the clouds is mentioned in the apocalyptic language of the last book in the Bible (Rev 4:3). This early instance of God's covenant with humankind will later be developed, renewed, and re-affirmed. The Greek word for *covenant* (*diatheke*) is also the word translated into English as *testament* (Old Testament, New Testament). This translation stresses that God's relationship with the world he created, and the manner in which matters stand between himself and his people lie at the heart of the scriptures.

In the next part of Genesis, from Chapter 12 to Chapter 50, the origins of Israel are described. This is the patriarchal period. The leading names of Abraham, Isaac, Jacob, and Joseph figure in close connection with the families, clans, and communities which surround them. These chapters provide the background to the Exodus from Egypt and the point where the history of Israel and the struggle of that nation to maintain its identity makes a firm beginning. Israel, which was at first a name for the patriarch Jacob, became afterwards the title of a people and a nation and, in due course, a promised land. The patriarchal period falls within the second millennium. The familiar names of Abraham, Jacob, Benjamin are found in texts discovered by archaeologists in Mesopotamia and Egypt, although there is no mention of the patriarchs of Genesis themselves.

This is an 'heroic age' and often the most ancient and reliable evidence of happenings at this time of world's history is found in poems, lists of names, and laws. The complete documents are themselves of a much later date. Such information was handed on orally, by groups and families, learnt by heart, and passed by word of mouth from generation to generation.

There are many gaps in the story. The aim of the collection of sagas is not historical, but religious. The theology of a church as 'a community called out' shines through the literary forms. The development of God's covenant (Gen 15, 17) gave the promise of 'the whole land of Canaan' to Abraham's family. He would be 'the father of a multitude of nations' and circumcision would mark the bodies of their descendants 'in perpetuity' (Gen 17:13). The social pattern was more complex than the narrative suggests. In addition to Abraham's family connection, ancestors of Moab, Ammon, and Edom (Gen 19:30-38; 25:1-5 and 12-18) were probably among those who swelled the numbers of this migrant, semi-nomadic people. The epic style seems to make the story more simple than in fact it was. There are some anachronisms in the editing and the later shaping of the text, e.g. there is a premature reference to Philistines who came to Palestine at a much later date (Gen 21:32-34 and also Gen 26).

Abraham may have come either from Ur 'in the land of the Chaldaeans' or else from upper Mesopotamia (Gen 11:31-12:10). It is from the north-western Semitic stock, with its mixture of many traditions, that Israel's ancestors came. The Arameans are descendants of Shem (Gen 10:21-31) through a line parallel to that of Eber, the traditional ancestor of the Hebrews. The Arameans and Chaldaeans according to Genesis 22:20-24 are the offspring of Abraham's brother, Nahor. The famous confessional creed of Deut 26:5 supports this: 'A wandering Aramean was my father'.

Some of the names in Genesis refer to individual personalities, others denote tribal groupings. Abraham's son Isaac is chiefly remembered for the incident in which the father is directed to sacrifice his son. The obedience of Abraham and the last minute rescue of Isaac mark another occasion for renewing the covenant. 'In thy seed shall all the nations of the earth be blessed; because thou hast obeyed my voice' (Gen 22:18).

Jacob, in contrast with Esau, is depicted, for all his faults, as the spiritual man. He is granted the vision at Bethel (Gen 28) after he has received the much-coveted blessing of his father, Isaac, although he was younger than Esau (Gen 27). After his long absence of twenty years in Aramean country, he faces, on his return, a physical and spiritual struggle at Peniel, the ford of the river Jabbok. This is both a moral test and a sign of his calling and his destiny to be the leader of his people. He is given a new name, Israel, 'for thou hast striven with God and with men, and hast prevailed' (Gen 32:28). The title Israel may mean 'may God show his strength'.

The story of Joseph has been called a 'novella'. There are no collection of incidents from various sources to be edited. Neither Joseph nor the Pharaoh who befriended him is mentioned in historical records apart from Genesis.

The conclusions of Genesis and the completion of the patriarchal period might sum up the significance of the whole book in the phrase 'the deliverance of a numerous people' (Gen 50:20).

The scene is now set for the story of Moses.

EXODUS

With the book of Exodus, we are given a glimpse of Egyptian history. The king of Egypt, the Pharaoh of the day, perhaps Ramses II (1290-1225 B.C.), enters the story of the Hebrew people. This was the unwelcoming Pharaoh who 'knew not Joseph' (Ex 1:8).

The way out from slavery became a continuing theme throughout the Bible. The deliverance and the journey to freedom and a promised land is told not only in Exodus, but was constantly remembered in after years at festivals such as the Passover. The psalmist (e.g. Psalm 77) praised God for the journey through the sea and the leading of the people like a flock 'by the hand of Moses and Aaron'. This was a living tradition and a regular cause of thanksgiving.

The book of Exodus in its present form is the work of several authors, with different strands of tradition arranged into a single narrative. The general aim of the book is religious, for there are many gaps left in the historical account. The misfortunes which befell the people, as well as their disobedience and rebellion, disclose fresh thinking about the God who brought them out to freedom and rescued the nation. In Exodus, chapter 3, the vision granted to Moses at the burning bush is a moment of truth of a very special kind. The words 'I am who I am' (Ex 3:14) has been given many interpretations. Some see their meaning as 'I will be what I will be', indicating that the full nature and glory of God will unfold as events take place. The Priestly account (Ex 6:2) distinguishes Abraham's vision of El-Shaddai, 'God Almighty', (Gen 17:1) from the Yahweh of Moses. Others emphasise the anonymity of God who shall be nameless, recalling the tradition that saw 'the naming' of a person or thing as the exercising of power over what was named. A third reflection on the 'I am' may arise, not from Hebrew practical thinking, but more probably from Greek philosophy. The Greek version of the Bible phrases it characteristically: 'I am the one who is' – God is reality, the Lord of all being.

After freedom from slavery has been gained, the Exodus proper began with the journey through the desert. Uncertainty hangs over the exact route: there is doubt about the point in the sea of Reeds (*Yam Suph* Ex 13:18) at which the crossing was made. Miriam's short song about 'the horse and rider' in the waves has that ring of authenticity, which songs and ballads often possess before history was written (Ex 15:1).

Also the particular part of Sinai country has not been fully identified. The mountain, variously called Sinai or Horeb, on which the law was given, has retained its significance and symbolism through the subsequent centuries.

Exodus 20 lists the laws given by God to humankind. They are moral directives rather than ceremonial regulations. They are practical and personal, illustrating justice, humanity, purity, reverence, and trust in personal relationships, as well as the importance of a worship which is spiritual, with an awareness of God's holiness. The ten commandments form a charter of freedom and deliverance.

It became clear on the journey that laws were needed. In addition, the covenant, which had been drafted in simpler terms in patriarchal days, was now ready for more clearly defined expression. The manner in which it was renewed and developed is influenced by the pressures under which the people as a nation were living and progressing.

The Covenant in one tradition (J) is confirmed by a meal (Ex 24:11) and in another (E) by the sprinkling of blood (Ex 24:8). In the 'P' tradition the glory of Yahweh denotes his presence among his people.

The Book of the Covenant (Ex 24:7), with parallels in the Codes of Hammurabi and the Hittites, dealt with common law, both civil and penal, with ritual, and social morality. Perhaps this is the earlier code of Hebrew law (Ex 21:23-25: 'eye for eye, tooth for tooth': here punishment is equal to the damage done, and there is a check on excessive revenge).

God's uniqueness is emphasised (cf Ex 15:11: 'who is like him among the gods') as is also his concern for the oppressed in Egypt. At the same time his separateness transcends and his unapproachability increases the awareness of his holiness, his 'otherness'.

At Sinai, Yahweh was seen as just and humane, opposing falsity, cruelty and oppression. All this teaching was developed and applied by the prophets.

Apostasy and rebellion break in (Ex 32) and the golden calf (or bull) was worshipped. This symbol of 'godhead' in an agricultural community was common in the ancient east. Such idolatry led to massacre (Ex 32:28), after the tablets of the Law were broken. The renewal of the covenant and tablets, and the famous 'Name' of Yahweh (Ex 34:6-7: 'a God of tenderness and compassion, slow to anger, rich in kindness and faithfulness' – although invisible: 'man shall not see me and live') underlined the goodness and severity of God.

The worship of the people's God led to the building of a sanctuary – a simple nomad's tent – a tent (tabernacle) of meeting (Ex 29:42). It sheltered 'the ark of the covenant'. The ark was a token of God's presence with his people, carried on wanderings and into battle, described in poetry as the 'throne' of Yahweh. The tribe of Levi looked after these furnishings. Aaron and the priests were ministers through whom God was made known to Israel (Ex 29:46).

The Exodus theme

The theme of the Exodus continues through the scriptures. Small wonder that the books of the Pentateuch were called the books of Moses, the outstanding leader, who not only brought the people out of darkness and slavery, but shaped the kind of society which they should have, when he gave them their laws by the grace and power of God.

The book may conveniently be divided into three parts:

1. Chapters 1-12:36: the birth of Moses, his vision at the Burning bush, oppression of Egypt, building bricks without straw, the plagues, the Passover.
2. Chapters 12:37-18: the Exodus, manna, and water from the rock.
3. Chapters 19-40: the covenant, ten commandments, the Tabernacle, the golden calf, Moses and the glorious Presence of the Lord, the Ark.

LEVITICUS

In this third book of the Pentateuch, there is a break in the story. Leviticus is concerned with legislation. The 'Priestly' writer is at work here. Even if some very ancient and primitive features about sacrifices and cleanliness are included in the compilations of laws and ritual requirements, the book is probably to be dated in the sixth century B.C. at the time of Israel's exile (e.g. Lev 26:34 'you are in the country of your enemies') in Babylon, to which reference will later be made.

There are allusions to the Exodus but the experience of the exile, far from the spiritual centre of Jerusalem, provides the occasion for setting out in writing the details of the ritual and ceremonial of the Temple and also the duties of the priests. The name and achievement of Moses bring inspiration when the nation lost its power and a lonely exile under foreign domination was the plight of people.

It is important to note that the chapters on sacrifices of various kinds were not merely legal in their tone. They also reflect the joy and fellowship brought to the worshippers. The burnt offerings (Lev 1-5) signified the strengthening of the relationship between worshipper and God; peace was made and freedom found in a way that laws by themselves could not accomplish.

The day of Atonement is described in the finest detail. On the tenth day of the seventh month 'atonement will be made – to cleanse you' (Lev 16:30). This day is still observed, although much of the procedure outlined in Leviticus can no longer be observed. The entry of the priest into the 'most Holy Place', the Holy of Holies, the offering of incense before the Mercy Seat (the atonement cover, Lev 16:14) and its sprinkling with blood, and the scapegoat for Azazel sent off into the wilderness are all described. Azazel was a goat-deity, a demon God (Enoch 6, 8, 10 calls him a leader of the fallen angels).

The day of Atonement was an occasion of cleansing both of priests (Lev 16:11-14) and of people (Lev 16:15-19) – all their sins were despatched into the wilderness. 'Do not work that day' (Lev 23:28).

Code of Holiness

The 'idea of the holy' is dealt with at length (Lev 19:1, 27:34). There are rules codified about animal sacrifices and the prohibition of eating blood, marriage laws and rules of chastity (Lev 18), penalties for violation of ritual laws (Lev 20). There is also a calendar drawn up: Sabbath, Passover (Lev 23), Festival of Weeks, Day of Atonement, Shewbread. The Lex Talionis is stated (Lev 24:17-21: 'fracture for fracture, eye for eye, tooth for tooth'). Note the constant repetition of 'I am the Lord'. This refrain serves as a constant reminder that the whole of the people's life is lived in fellowship with a holy God (Lev 19:1).

Sacrifice is the offering of a material, especially a living, creature to God. In a 'peace offering' the worshipper shared in the flesh. In the 'burnt' offering (Lev 1) none of the flesh was eaten. Grain offerings (Lev 2) were also given to maintain the relationship with God. After the exile, during which sacrifices had temporarily ceased in the one sanctuary of Jerusalem, the ritual traditions were safeguarded, modified, and codified under the control of the Levitical priesthood and were embodied in their final form in Leviticus.

The people's sins included (1) pagan practices (2) social injustices and (3) political experiences.

They also committed sins of omission (Lev 5:1: 'because he does
not speak up when he hears a public charge to testify regarding
something he has seen or learned about, he will be held responsible').

The framework of Sinai appears artificial. Yet the sense of past
history were strong: 'These are the decrees the Lord established
on Mount Sinai (Lev 26:46)'; 'these were the commands the Lord
gave Moses on Mount Sinai for the Israelite' (Lev 27:34).

Leviticus: 5 Sections

1.	1-7:	the Law of Sacrifice.
2.	8-10:	inauguration of worship:
		Aaron consecrated.
3.	11-16:	the Law of Purification:
		Day of Atonements's cleansing.
4.	17-26:	the Law of Holiness.
		(cf Dead Sea Scrolls, Manual of Discipline).
5.	27:	vows and tithes.

NUMBERS

The book of Numbers receives its name from the Greek translation, as is the case with all the Pentateuch titles. A special emphasis is laid on the two census lists. The list of names underlines the continuity of the chosen people's history.

The Hebrew name for this book of the Torah is more colourful.
'In the wilderness' is the phrase, taken from the opening sentence to serve as a title.

This is not simple history. The importance of Numbers lies in the
teaching that is derived from the events. The progress and the
set-backs indicate the faithfulness of God in spite of the rebellious heart of the people whom he loves with protective caring.

These two themes run through both J's narrative and the Priestly
interpretation of the historical happenings.

J shows, with the gift, almost Homeric, of epic writing, that the
course of Israel's history is significant because at every turn it re-
lates the people to God. The framework seems to be influenced

at times by the calendar; what happens on the way is linked to the festivals: Exodus in terms of Passover, creation and the feast of Tabernacles, Sinai's covenant with the feast of Weeks.

The Priestly narrative, as might be expected, draws attention to the worship of the temple where God's presence is centred, from which his glory radiates. The writer's thoughts go back to the Tent of Meeting. Details of sacrifices, offerings, and the 'Red Cow' (Num 19:2) are recalled hundreds of years after these events.

DEUTERONOMY

Familiar ground is covered in the book of Deuteronomy. The days of wandering in the wilderness under the leadership of Moses are reviewed centuries later. The law is expressed afresh to suit the needs and problems of Israel, now an organised nation.

Deuteronomy, a Greek title, denotes not so much 'a second law' as 'a second edition of the law'. It might also refer to 'the copy of the law' (Deut 17:18), recalling the finding of the book of the law in the reign of King Josiah (622 B.C.: 2 Kgs 22.)

In this book, the teaching of Moses has been enlarged as a result of the influence of the prophets. It provides a pattern of daily life for those who lived in towns and villages. Probably it was not finally edited until about 300 B.C. with the revision carried out by the Priestly writers (Deut. 31:26).

As a book of the Bible, it has been called 'pivotal'. It may be better understood not only as the last book of the Pentateuch, but also as the first book of all that is contained in the writings which follow as far as 2 Kings.

In Deuteronomy, the law is less like a contract but has rather the character of a covenant. There is a note of warm love in the relationship of God with his chosen people (Deut 7:6). The spirit of Hosea fills some of the phrasing. The nearness of God is emphasised. (Deut 4:7)

Scholars have concluded that Deuteronomy is to be dated from the seventh century, since echoes of the eighth-century prophets can be traced through the text. The message of justice for the oppressed, for example, is loud and clear.

The 'discovery' of the book encouraged a new consistency in the disciplines and worship of the people. The importance of a central sanctuary at Jerusalem in the Temple became evident in the face of Canaanite religious practices. The attack made bravely and persistently by the prophets on idolatry may well account for the study in depth of the nature of idol-worship (see especially chapter 8; also 4:24; 12:5; 13).

The style of Deuteronomy is hortatory more than legalistic. The teaching is communicated through the sermon. There are traces of credal statements which encapsulate in words of worship the essentials of Israel's theology (Deut 6:4-9 and 26:5-10).

The environment of the Canaanite religion colours the style and presentation of the law of Moses. Deuteronomy tells of the oneness of the Lord, and the holiness of Israel. One sanctuary conserves this unity; one priesthood and one book control the doctrine and life.

An interesting revision of the fourth commandment is revealing. In Deut 5:15 the observance of the sabbath is linked with the Exodus and not with the Creation as in Ex 20. A philosophy of history emerges in this narrative of the Deuteronomic writer. In chapters 1-16, history is outlined and its significance for the chosen people is expounded.

Chapters 12-26 set out the code of behaviour which claims the obedience of the people. Not only must they resist the pressures put upon them to serve other gods (Deut 13), but they must show tenderness and mercy to those who are poor and deprived (Deut 24:10-22). They were to show solidarity with foreigners dwelling in exile in their land (Deut 10:19, 23:7).

In Deuteronomy, the richness of the word 'covenant' is disclosed. Covenant is a kind of life. The breaking of a covenant with God is death, for the relationship with the creator, the Lord of all life, is broken. 'Choose life' (Deut 30:19) seems to sum up the message of the writer.

It is not surprising to find that Jesus quotes from Deuteronomy more frequently than from any other Old Testament book. The old truths are presented with a striking freshness. The new Exodus, and a new covenant which is inward and personal, are thoughts probably inspired by Jeremiah who wrote of a remnant, returning not from Egypt but from another exile, to their own land (Jer 23 and 31:31). A new look on the nation's heritage, as outlined by the prophets, makes Deuteronomy's words carry an authority of considerable weight for the future of Israel's national life.

CHAPTER 4

The Historical Books

The Early Prophets

The Books of Joshua, Judges, Samuel (1 & 2), and Kings (1 & 2) are called the 'Early Prophets' in the Hebrew Bible; Ruth is excepted. The 'Later Prophets' are Isaiah, Jeremiah, Ezekiel, and the 12 minor prophets. Daniel is later still, with an increased measure of apocalyptic teaching.

These historical books were written from a religious standpoint. Joshua and Samuel dominate as they communicate the word of the Lord to the people of Israel and make the relationship between God and the people their prime concern.

Other prophets besides Samuel are involved in the history; although their writings are not evident, the words of Gad, Nathan, Elijah and Elisha have significant influence. The Book of Kings also provides the social and historical background for the major 'writing' prophets, Isaiah and Jeremiah.

The link between the Law and the 'early prophets' is to be found in Deuteronomy 34:9 where it is recorded that Moses before his death had laid his hands on Joshua who 'was filled with the spirit of wisdom'. Deuteronomy supplies the basis for the 'choosing' by God of the people and Joshua gives effect to their chosen-ness by leading them into the promised land and establishing them there.

The Book of Judges tells a story of failures and set-backs, yet Israel's identity is not lost; restorations and recoveries form part of the chequered pattern of victory and defeat.

Monarchy and the role of David are the themes of the Books of Samuel; in the Books of Kings, starting from the reign of Solomon, there is more disobedience in the nation and much infidelity on the part of the leaders in spite of some shining royal exceptions. God's judgement makes history.

In the compilation of this history, there are signs of various editors at work upon the oral traditions from which they set down the narrative in writing. It seems clear to the scholars that, with hindsight in succeeding centuries, these meditations upon the nation's history and the religious lessons to be drawn from the events were paramount in the narrative. This is not to denigrate the historicity; references, documentary and archaeological, from non-biblical sources can sometimes be used to corroborate the details of what took place. Yet the narratives are clearly selective. For example, the scanty references to Omri, who built Samaria, scarcely do justice to the importance of that monarch.

JOSHUA

After the Pentateuch, the book of Joshua is the first of the group of writings called in the Hebrew Bible 'the former or the early Prophets'. Clearly there is a blend of prophecy and history. The book interprets the events recorded and explains their religious meaning. Prophecy is concerned with a pointing to the significance of what actually happens to the people; at other times the prophets looked ahead into the future.

Joshua, whose very name signified 'salvation', exercises his role as the successor of Moses. He has been given the leadership and with this authority he continues the story of the Exodus and the deliverance from Egyptian slavery and darkness. There are striking parallels which recall the achievement of Moses. The crossing of Jordan recalls the marvel of the crossing of the Red Sea (Jos 3:13). The symbolism of the 'ark of the covenant' containing the law, and the twelve representatives leading the way, is a reminder of God's ordering and choice in all that occurs.

Twelve stones indicated that in Gilgal the promise of a land of their own was fulfilled. Circumcision, passover, milk and honey instead of manna explained the fact that the Exodus was accomplished and Jordan was crossed (chapter 5).

There was, however, much work to be done. Jericho's collapse was indeed astonishing. The next objective Ai was taken too, after near disaster caused by a hint of rebellion and a reluctance among the people, already over-confident. Joshua's spiritual leadership was sorely needed for military success in the tasks of conquest. Southern cities, as well as northern, form the opposition; this contrast between north and south smacks of the chronicler's hindsight when the full history came to be recorded.

The whole land was not entirely conquered. A spiritual centre, however, was set up, first at Shiloh, then at Shechem. The religious emphasis was carried into the apportionment of land, when the Levites, whose inheritance was God and not land, instead of receiving an apportionment, were allocated centres throughout the whole confederation.

Before the death of Joshua and his burial, the farewell speech indicates the meaning and purpose of his life. He was God's agent; he urged the people to obey God's commandments; he discouraged any association or assimilation with the neighbouring nations, since their gods were false.

Intermarriage, for example, was strictly forbidden. This would spell disaster. The people must hold to the covenant and remember their history and inheritance, especially Abraham and Moses, their calling and deliverance.

The Book of Joshua can readily be divided into three parts:

1-12	Conquest of Promised land
13-21	Partition of the land among the tribes; the cities of refuge; the cities of the Levites
22-24	Joshua's farewell speech and death at Shechem.

JUDGES

The Book of Judges, following Joshua, continues the story of the settlement of Israel in Palestine during the two centuries after 1225 B.C.

The history interprets in religious terms the fortunes of the people. There is almost a liturgical ring about such phrases as 'the land had rest for 40 years' when the battles were over with some victories won and God was praised. Scholars see the hand of a 'deuteronomic' writer in the rhetoric of some of the records. Although the narrative is not straight-forward history, there are lessons for the nation to learn from the story told in epic style.

Judges bridges the period between the death of Joshua and the beginning of the monarchy. A judge was counted as a leader and ruler of the country. The problems which they encountered are set out in religious terms (2:11-19). When Israel succumbs to the temptation 'to serve Baal and Ashtaroth', the nation suffers divine punishment. Archaeologists have shown that the Canaanites were more sophisticated and advanced in civilisation than was, until recently, popularly supposed; their gods had a subtle attraction for the Israelites.

Israel's desire to integrate was apparently strong. When the people repent, however, and give their allegiance once more to the God of Israel, they are delivered from the enemy.

'Whenever the Lord raised up judges for them, the Lord was with the judge and he saved them from the hands of their enemies all the days of the judge – but, whenever the judge died, they turned back and behaved worse than their fathers, going after other gods, serving them and bowing down to them' (2:18-19).

The judges are praised in the book of Ecclesiasticus (Ecclus 46:11-12); their hearts did not fall into idolatry; they did not turn away from the Lord. They are commended also, as a group, in the impressive chapter on faith in the New Testament (Hebrews 11). Gideon, Barak, Samson, and Jephthah are listed before David and Samuel for their conquest of kingdoms through faith. They did what was right, earning the promises. 'They were weak people who were given strength' (Heb 11:34).

The last words of Judges (21:25) refer to the independence of the tribes. 'There was no king, and everyone did what was right in his own eyes.'

The judge was a champion, rather than a legal figure. Often these leaders were vivid, charismatic personalities.

If Joshua lays stress upon the power and grace of God through the occupation of the promised land and in the covenant, Judges illustrates the discipline which God imposes on his people (Jos 23) and paves the way towards the future monarchy.

RUTH

'In the days of the judges'. With these words begins a short story full of charm and family feeling. The book of Ruth has also been called a miniature novel, with three main characters, Ruth and her mother-in-law, Naomi, and Boaz whom Ruth eventually married.

This is a book about people and their relationships. It also throws light on radical tensions and the manner in which they can be overcome. Furthermore, it illustrates family law, its obligations, rights of succession, and rights of redemption.

Ruth's first husband died. She, a Moabitess, had married into a family from Bethlehem in Judah. As a young widow, she was ready to return there with her mother-in-law Naomi. 'Your people shall be my people', Ruth said to the hesitant mother-in-law.

There follows a vivid description of Ruth in the corn-fields of Boaz, her late husband's kinsman (2:1). As a poor person, she was permitted to glean. Ruth is noticed and appreciated, although a foreigner. She gleaned diligently, and gathered enough barley for Naomi and herself.

The upshot is that Boaz, encouraged by Naomi, marries Ruth. Technicalities of family law are settled when Boaz (4:8) purchases the right of redemption from the one who was heir to the land belonging to Naomi's husband Elimelech. Ruth was included in the purchase (4:10). Boaz became the 'goel', the one who, as next-of-kin, had the right to redeem.

Boaz and Ruth had a son Obed who became the father of Jesse, who in turn had a son David. Thus David's great-grandmother had been a Moabitess. The short story gives a glimpse of flexibility and tolerance, such as is expressed in the later chapters of Isaiah and in Jonah.

The Book of Ruth in the Hebrew Scriptures is placed among the five scrolls used for reading at the major festivals. Ruth, appropriately, is read at the end of the harvest. Ruth, as one of the Writings, was accepted at a later stage into the Jewish canon and is thought to belong to the time of the exile. Ruth's name appears in St Matthew's genealogy (Mt 1:5).

I AND II SAMUEL

The 'sacred history' continues. After the chequered fortunes of the nation in the period of the Judges, the prophet Samuel becomes the instrument for the establishment of the monarchy.

The two books of Samuel, originally a single book, trace the significant events from the rise of the monarchy to the close of the reign of David in the eleventh and tenth centuries B.C. In the LXX with 1 & 2 Kings they were called the four Books of the Reigns. There are five distinct sections:

1. The story of Samuel
2. Samuel and Saul
3. Saul and David
4. David
5. Appendices

David alone reached the ideal and became the type of the expected Messiah, since Saul had been a failure and David's successors were wayward and disobedient. Many 'did that which was evil'.

Samuel's life is dated about 1050 B.C. The enemies facing Israel at the time were the Philistines. They had come from Crete and settled along the coast of Palestine. (The name Palestine is derived from these inhabitants of Philistia.) They were armed with iron weapons; the bronze age was ending.

Israel's unity was an important factor in the nation's history. The common worship of their God was one way which helped bond racial solidarity. There was a distinct charisma about the 'ark' as a rallying point in a 'holy war'. This was especially marked at a time when there was no permanence in the leadership, no right of succession. Politically, growing population and pressure on the land from the Philistines put in question the long-term viability of the less central leadership structures of the period of the judges. Soon the desire for a king and a monarchy became more urgent.

Samuel grew up in the sanctuary of Shiloh. He also continued the work of Moses as a leader. He reunited the people after the up-and-down experiences of the judges and the zig-zag progress of the people's fortunes.

Samuel came at a lean time, spiritually speaking. There was no open vision. In fact, the 'evil' of corruption and decline was all too threatening. Under Samuel, after the fall of Shiloh at the hands of hostile Philistines, the people rallied at Mizpah, the covenant with Yahweh was renewed and the enemy driven back. Samuel was a religious and political reformer. He was part prophet, part judge; he was also called 'seer'.

There were many ugly incidents as well. Personalities such as those of Joel and Abijah, the sons of Samuel, were considered to be power-hungry. The people clamoured for a king. Samuel was a reluctant king-maker, but, as if under pressure, he agreed to anoint Saul from the tribe of Benjamin, with evident misgiving. He thought that the people would lose their independence and liberty.

Saul, who perhaps reigned for some 10-12 years, was a military leader rather than a statesmanlike king. With David as king, the nation had a ruler to help the people to fulfil their destiny. He established a centre at Jerusalem and thus gave leadership to Judah. David's reign lasted from c. 1010-970. Jerusalem, where he built his palace (2 Sam 5), became a symbol of political unity and the religious capital of the nation. He brought the ark to Jerusalem (2 Sam 6) and at last the Philistines were defeated (2 Sam 21). The story of his reign is told in vivid, often poetical, language. The weaknesses of the king, evident often in the disorders and troubles in his own family, are included: tragedy and triumph are interwoven. The death of his son Absalom revealed the depth of David's finest feelings, when he cried out 'would God I had died for thee, O Absalom, my son, my son' (2 Sam 19:4)

The poems in these two books of Samuel are important ancient sources. They reveal in language of great beauty the strong traditions surrounding the nation's history. Hannah's prayer, (1 Sam 2:1-10) 'the Lord will judge the ends of the earth' (verse 10), is full of confidence in the future.

David's lament over Saul and Jonathan (2 Sam 1) is tender and generous in the face of deep sorrow. Another moving lament over Abner, the military commander, (2 Sam 3) bears the marks of 'the sweet singer of Israel'.

The 'last words of David' (2 Sam 23:1-7) unfold the meaning of ideal kingship exercised under the guidance of the Most High God: 'has he not made with me an everlasting covenant?' (verse 5).

I AND II KINGS

The two books of Kings were originally one. They were separated by the Greek translator, who named them '3rd and 4th Kingdoms'. The books of Samuel were called '1st and 2nd Kingdoms'.

1 Kings

The story of kingship in Israel develops after the death of David. Solomon, his son, succeeds and the monarchy becomes hereditary.

A period of building and administration follows the former tale of military conquests. Solomon was no soldier. For him there was an urgent concern to establish Jerusalem as a centre worthy of the worship of God. The construction of the Temple was a seven-year-long building programme (6:38). In it the ark of the covenant was placed (8:6). The great prayer of dedication assured all that God's 'name' was there (8:43).

The Hall of Judgement and the Royal Palace are also described in careful detail. The glory and the grandeur of the capital city, however, proved costly. Materials of timber (5:6), stone (5:17), and precious metals, including pure gold (6:21) were imported. The political situation favoured such elaborate planning and, in particular, the friendly Phoenician co-operation from Hiram, king of Tyre (5), made the prestigious undertaking possible. The people, on the other hand, had to face necessary taxation to meet the full cost (5:13). Hiram received wheat and oil in return for his magnificent trees (5:11). Later there is mention of the ceding of twenty Galilean cities to the Tyrian king (9:11). Forced labour added to the people's burden (5:13). Solomon organised the collection of contributions from the whole country, marked off into twelve regions for this purpose (4:7-19). There was the feeling among the tribes that Judah was receiving special treatment. The seeds of division were already being sown, even while 'all the glory' associated with Solomon's reign was winning the admiration of neighbouring countries. The queen of Sheba's appreciation, colourfully told, became proverbial.

Solomon's marriage with the daughter of an Egyptian Pharaoh

(3:1) improved relationships on the south-west borders with that great power (9:16). In the north, the defeat of the Hittite empire and the peaceful lull on the international scene, before the emergence of the threat from Assyria, enabled the king to have favourable conditions for the embellishment of the city.

The narrative emphasises the wisdom of the king and sheds lustre on his devotion to God. The high standard of worship and the increased awareness of God's holiness found expression in the architecture and detailed design of the temple.

The story was set down in writing and shaped in its final form long after. The authorship is understood to be 'deuteronomic': those who were responsible for the editing of the historical events looked upon the nation of Israel, from the point of view of the compilers of Deuteronomy, as first and foremost a covenant people, 'a holy nation'. The political details which were recorded always had a religious point. The 'covenant theme' was predominant. There were sources mentioned such as the annals of Solomon, the annals of the Kings of Israel, and the annals of the Kings of Judah. It is clearly shown in the final form of this history that the Canaanties, on account of their 'fertility cults' and pagan civilisation, were a danger to Israel's faith and morals.

Hence it was concluded that Solomon's reign had very mixed results. His achievement was there for all to see and an admitted success. Yet, the legacy left by the king was marked by strife, discontent, and open rebellion. In such a complex situation, the close of Solomon's reign was a story of failing influence; his foreign wives (11:4) illustrated his flouting of the law forbidding such associations; his oppressive government had disappointed those who had initially welcomed a monarchy in their longing for stability and prosperity.

After Solomon's death (11:43), Rehoboam succeeded. Only two tribes, however, Judah and Benjamin, remained loyal to him. Two kingdoms resulted: Judah in the south and Israel in the north.

Jeroboam as king of this Israel revived local worship. He set up a ceremony of calf-worship in Dan and Bethel as a counter-attraction to the feasts and ceremonies in Jerusalem (12:25-33).

The prophets condemned these practices. They were reactionary and contrary to the law of Moses. Jeroboam was repeatedly referred to as the king 'who made Israel to sin'.

Of the kings which followed, Omri had particular significance. He founded a dynasty at Samaria and is mentioned on the Moabite stone of King Mesha. This record of the Moabite king's victories against Israel has survived; discovered in 1868 at Dibon (modern Dhiban, east of the Dead Sea), it is now in the Paris Louvre. Omri himself receives somewhat scant attention in Kings, although the Assyrian name for Israel in inscriptions was 'the land of Omri'.

The rest of Kings recounts the events of Omri's son Ahab. With Ahab's death about the year 853 B.C., the book concludes.

The role of Elijah in his struggle with Ahab and in his championing of the worship of Yahweh in the face of the gods worshipped by the Canaanites and the Phoenicians (18) marks him out as one of the greatest of the Hebrew prophets. His stand for moral uprightness and social justice are frequently quoted. The manner of his departure from this world (2 Kgs 2:1-18) encouraged a belief in his return with messianic powers.

2 Kings

The story of the nation when divided moves to and fro, now in the north, now in the south. The threat of Assyria brought the kingdoms together for a time (1 Kgs 22:29) when Ahab, King of Israel, and Jehoshaphat, King of Judah, formed an alliance. The defeat of the Assyrians at Qarqar in 853 is not recorded in the Bible: clearly the Syrian forces joining with Ahab and Jehoshaphat held the Assyrians in check and hindered their advance towards that other great power in Egypt. This was part of political history.

The writer of 2 Kings, however, is concerned more particularly with the religious message of the prophets. Incidents in the life of Elisha following upon his predecessor Elijah are told at length (2 Kgs 4-6). Both prophets illustrate the tensions which existed between their way of life and their moral standards on the one hand and the general disloyalty of the kings on the other. Elisha is a paler personality than Elijah. Elijah's strong character and attractive independence of mind made his message searching and thrustful. Elisha appears rather as one of a group of prophets. The adventures of both appear to have been collected from an independent source, separate from the annals of the kings.

The kings whose reigns are described with special commendation are Hezekiah and Josiah. The majority of the monarchs are reported as evil-doers in the sight of the Lord. Hezekiah (2 Kgs 18), although politically ineffective, was a religious reformer and showed much concern for the Temple and its worship. The remarkable incident of Sennacherib's withdrawal with his hostile Assyrian forces is interpreted as a sign of Jerusalem's inviolability (2 Kgs 19:32-34). Isaiah the prophet made this clear.

Josiah stands out in this history as a timely reformer (2 Kgs 22-23). The prophets, such as Zephaniah (Zeph 3:1) and Jeremiah (Jer 2:13), had pointed out the social injustices and moral corruption that prevailed. The discovery of 'the law' by Hilkiah the high priest disturbed the king deeply. This 'law' may have been part of Deuteronomy or a similar document. It certainly stirred Josiah to take urgent steps to abolish idolatry and to centralise the worship of God in Jerusalem. The local sanctuaries were demolished and the spiritual quality of worship improved. The Law was seen to be the basis of the social and religious life of the nation.

Scholars conclude that these books of Kings (1 and 2) were drawn up to be read by those who were exiled in Babylon in the years that followed 586 B.C. Through the turbulent events, the dangers and the battles, the people were enabled to see that they had a distinct identity and were chosen for a destiny. They were God's people and therefore pure and true worship must have priority in the national life. The narrative is repeatedly concerned with the dilemma facing the citizens: whether to be in the world with the kings, or not entirely of the world with the prophets.

I AND II CHRONICLES

The books of Chronicles stand last in the Hebrew Old Testament.

No one knows for certain who the chronicler was. Some have suggested Ezra as the writer. Chronicles together with the books of Ezra and Nehemiah form a tripartite volume. The end of 2

Chronicles is repeated in the book of Ezra (2 Chr 36:22-23 equals Ezra 1:1-3).

At any rate, the chronicler may well have been in Jerusalem about the year 300 B.C. Apparently he had a special interest in the music of the Temple (1 Chr 16).

The Temple had been rebuilt. Haggai and Zechariah had heralded this with rejoicing; the walls of the city were restored under the supervision of Nehemiah; the law had become a national charter, thanks to the work of Ezra.

Israel's history at this stage is marked by much less conflict and controversy. Political life is exchanged for a strict and well-ordered religious life. The Chronicler appears to be selective in his presentation of the historical facts. The emphasis is upon the fortunes of Judah and little mention is made of Israel, the northern kingdom.

1 Chronicles

The first nine chapters consist of genealogical lists. The emphasis is on Judah. These family trees and lines of descendants are drawn up to indicate the existing social and religious structure of the nation. There are certain omissions: Seth is mentioned as the second name after Adam (1 Chr 1:1). Neither Cain nor Abel is included. The list of the Semites, the sons of Shem, leads into the family of Abraham (1 Chr 1:17; 27). Judah's disasters are mentioned in 1 Chr 2:3, 7.

Chapters 10-29 deal with the history of David. The conflict and quarrel with Saul are not mentioned. The Bathsheba incident is omitted. David is portrayed, not so much as a warrior, but as the one who was chosen and reigned as king in the specially selected place where the Temple was sited and built in Jerusalem. Nathan is prominent as a prophet. A detailed description of the Ark and the bringing of it to Jerusalem is highlighted (1 Chr 13, 15). Preparations for the Temple under David's planning are described in chapter 22. David's prayer is phrased with a solemn beauty in chapter 29:10-13.

2 Chronicles

The first nine chapters deal with Solomon and the building of the Temple, including the dedication (chapter 7). The queen of

Sheba is attracted by the splendour of it all (chapter 9) as is described in 1 Kgs 10.

The importance of the continuity of the nation's history is stressed. Also the religious meaning of the events is underlined, even if not all events are included.

There is only a single mention of Elijah (2 Chr 21:12) from whom Jehoram King of Judah received a letter. Jehoram is coupled with Ahab; both are held responsible for leading the people astray. Elisha is not mentioned at all.

EZRA AND NEHEMIAH

The two books of Ezra and Nehemiah are more likely 'memoirs' than historical narrative. Closely linked with the Books of Chronicles, they supply valuable evidence for the development of the life and society of the Jewish people on their return from exile.

Cyrus, king of Persia, issued his edict in 538 B.C. which permitted the Jews to return to Jerusalem. This Cyrus was 'the shepherd' named in the prophecy (Is 44:28) as the one who would bring deliverance and give the order for Jerusalem and the Temple to be rebuilt. Cyrus may also have had his own reasons for maintaining good relationships with the Jewish people, in case Egypt should threaten.

Accordingly, the Jews were allowed to take back the sacred vessels of the temple and to rebuild the ruined sanctuary. The joy of the people was ecstatic (Ezra 3:10). However, controversy soon clouded the scene, since the people of Samaria, who were not welcomed as helpers in the rebuilding, began to interfere with the progress of the work (Ezra 4:1-3). The prophet Haggai (Hag 1:2) pointed to the people's indifference about the rebuilding, and spurred on the work which was of very great importance as a symbol of unity and a visible spiritual centre. The Temple was completed in 516 B.C.

At this time, the title 'High Priest' began to be used and the formation of an ecclesiastical dynasty took place in Judah. Yet there was widespread despondency during the sixty years that followed: the tolerance of inter-marriage with outsiders endangered Judaism's identity. Malachi reflects the mood of the time and a nucleus of those 'who feared the Lord' (Mal 3:16), dismayed at the trend of events, welcomed the arrival of Ezra in 458 B.C. Artaxerxes, after the disasters experienced by the Persians in Greece at Marathon in 490 and Salamis in 480, deemed it prudent to encourage Ezra to go to Judaea, for the sake of peace in the whole area.

Ezra went with the Book of the Law which had been enlarged and edited during the exile. He dealt strictly with the marriage problem: alien wives were to be put away (Ezra 10). The task of rebuilding the walls of the city, after all the set-backs, was taken in hand effectively when Nehemiah arrived as governor. Nehemiah, who had the confidence of Artaxerxes as the king's cupbearer, was able with the assistance of Persian troops to check their opponents' policy of hindering the work. The building continued for fifty-two days; the wall and the gates were finished in 444 B.C.; then followed the dedication (Neh 12:27).

The public reading of the Law was a significant ceremony. Ezra at the Water-gate 'translated and gave the sense' of the Law so that the people understood what was read (Neh 8:8). This continued for seven days: the people broke down in tears, but were told by Ezra and Nehemiah not to grieve (Neh 8:9).

The covenant was renewed between Israel and Yahweh: not only did the people undertake to abstain from intermarriage, they also pledged themselves to observe the sabbath and the feast days with strict care. Everyone was to give one third of a shekel yearly to defray the expenses of the temple worship (Neh 10:32).

This was a turning point in the nation's history. The Law now became the people's book and was not for the priests alone. It served as a great bond between all in the dispersion.

Nehemiah returned to Persia for a year in 433 B.C. When he came back to Jerusalem he found problems of laxity and neglect in worship and conduct in spite of his efforts to improve social and financial conditions for the people. His prayer reveals his disappointment and the gentle love and concern which characterised his work for the citizens: 'Remember me for this, my God,' he prayed, 'Do not blot out the pious deed I have done for the temple of my God and its liturgy' (Neh 13:14).

ESTHER

This dramatic story in a Persian setting illustrates the remarkable ability of the Jewish people to survive in the face of fierce opposition. In the historical framework of the reign of Xerxes (Ahasuerus), King of Persia 485-465 B.C., the events take place in the royal capital of Susa (Sushan the Palace).

Esther's name, in the book's title, may actually be less important than that of her uncle, Mordecai. Together, however, as members of the Jewish population, living in exile far from their homeland, they receive the support of the King for their nation. Although the name of God is not specifically mentioned in the Hebrew version of the story, there are two significant sentences which hint strongly that the Jews, through all the controversy and conflict concerning their presence among the Persians, were in a special way guided and protected as a nation with a destiny. When Mordecai, the leader and spokesman of the Jewish community, urges his niece Queen Esther to tell the King, whose favour she enjoys, that there is a plot to assassinate their people, he says 'Who knows whether it is not for such a time as this that you have come to royal estate?' (4:14: NEB). Furthermore, when the wife of Haman, the would-be persecutor, sensing the coming failure of the plot, says to her husband, 'If Mordecai, in face of whom your fortunes begin to fall, belongs to the Jewish race, you will not get the better of him; he will see your utter downfall' (6:13 NEB), then the destiny and future survival of the Jewish nation are seen to have a certain inevitability.

Only at a late stage was the book listed in the Jewish canon. Likewise, the Christian Church scarcely referred to it in the early centuries. There was a longer version in the Greek LXX: six additions were inserted at different points in the story and were placed by Jerome in his Latin Vulgate Bible at the end of the Book of Esther. These six passages make frequent reference to God and the element of prayer is made prominent. These additions to the Book of Esther have a place in the Apocrypha.

The festival of Purim (or 'lots') may have been the reason for the inclusion of the story of Esther in the scriptures. In 9:20-32 Mordecai's account of the annual celebration by the Jews on the fourteenth and fifteenth of the month Adar (March) commemorates the great release from their enemies.

The date of the book may be placed in the early part of the second century B.C. in Palestine. The 'addition' mentions that the Letter of Purim (11:1) was brought to Egypt in the fourth year of the reign of Ptolemy and Cleopatra (114-113 B.C.).

CHAPTER 5

The Wisdom Books and the Psalms

JOB

Job is mentioned in the book of Ezekiel (Ez 14:14) together with Noah and Daniel. These three names are quoted as typical examples of righteousness.

Later, perhaps between 450 and 350 B.C., the book of Job was written and is now renowned as a piece of 'wisdom' literature. There is no reference to Israel or the history of the nation. The problem, with which it deals in dramatic dialogue and colourful poetry, concerns God's government of the world and the relationship between God and humankind.

In the prologue (1-2) the affluent life of Job and his family is described in six scenes. This man, both prosperous and above reproach as a citizen, is apparently to be challenged and tested by 'satanic' action. Disasters are reported. Job's herds and other property are destroyed. His house is wrecked by storm damage; his children are killed in the process. Job remains steadfast through this grim experience. He says in words which still have a familiar ring: 'The Lord gave and the Lord has taken away: blessed be the name of the Lord'(1:21). His wife recommends that he should give in to this calamity. 'Curse God and die,' she says, but Job, convinced of his innocence, replies, 'If we take happiness from God's hands, must we not take sorrow, too?' (2:10).

Three friends, Eliphaz, Bildad, and Zophar, come to him in an attempt to comfort and condole with him. They are silent until Job speaks.

In the poetic dialogue which follows, the heroic Job, who has displayed exceptional fortitude, reveals the extent of the agonising, the perplexity, and the questioning through which he is passing. In the end, his faith triumphs; he does not attempt to justify himself.

When he speaks, Job expresses his feelings by wishing he had never been born. Eliphaz, his first comforter, thinks that something has gone wrong. Man is born to trouble. 'I would appeal to God,' he suggests (5:8).

Job feels that Eliphaz is not helping. Job, asserting innocence, agonises, finding his days have no meaning (6:30; 7:16).

Bildad, the second comforter, intervenes saying that God does not pervert justice (8:3). Job resents that his friends do not think him innocent. He longs for some means of arbitration (9:33).

Zophar adds a rough remark about Job's idle talk (11:3) and questions whether Job can fathom the mysteries of God (11:7). To which Job replies, with some impatience, 'Doubtless you are the people' (12:1).

Before the second round of conversation, Job cries out that, even if God slays him, he will trust in him (13:15). He reflects on the shortness of life (14:1); he muses: 'If a man dies, will he live again?' (14:14).

Eliphaz comes in again with more rebukes than comfortable words. Bildad asks Job to bring an end to his speech-making. Job senses a deep loneliness but holds on to his convictions. 'I have escaped by only the skin of my teeth,' (19:20) he cries. 'I know that my redeemer liveth' (19:25). Zophar's intervention refers in grisly language to the fate that God assigns to the wicked (20:29). Job protests, 'Why should I not be impatient?' (21:4).

The third round of comforting is of no help. Eliphaz still thinks that Job is wicked. Bildad adds that man is only a worm (25:6). Job persists, 'I will maintain my righteousness' (27:6).

The rich poetry of his monologue about searching for God as miners search for gold (28-31) is a highlight in the book.

Then, rather awkwardly, the speeches of Elihu are inserted (32–37). These may have been added at a later date. Although a younger man than 'the comforters', he argues at great length that the suffering is remedial: 'we learn' through it all (36:10).

Then God appears and demonstrates that he is master of the forces of evil (38-41). Vivid illustrations of the whirlwind, the hippopotamus, and the crocodile affirm God's almightiness in and over creation. Job has his eyes opened and, in repentance, he holds fast to God (42:5, 6). The Epilogue pictures Job with fortunes restored and increased and a long life ahead.

The questions raised in the book of Job are asked by human beings in every age. Of their complexity there is no doubt. The book of Job may not disclose the reason why people suffer, but it certainly reveals the power of faith, given by God, to a person nearly overcome by devastating disasters of the most personal kind, but sustained patiently, with understandable periods of impatience, by his trust in God. The endurance of Job, in the face of mockery, scepticism, and hostile criticism, is admirable and exemplary. He learned the meaning of faith by the hard way of abandonment and near despair.

THE PSALMS

Both Jews and Christians have used the psalms regularly in services of public worship. They have also found in them a treasure-house of spiritual riches.

They express in the language of poetry the mystery of worship and the experience of the individual as well as of a church in relationship with God.

The psalms are often called the psalms of David. Some of the psalms in the collection of one hundred and fifty may have been written by David. He may also have inspired others to compose psalms. Even so, the final form of the Psalter was not reached before the second century B.C. The collection is 'Davidic' in the sense that the tradition associated with David (1 Sam 16:17-23, 2 Sam 1:17-27 and Amos 6:5) is maintained long after his time. It is thought that David-like psalms belong to the first half, and anonymous psalms are in the second half.

After the return from captivity in Babylon, with the renewing and strengthening of temple worship from 538 B.C. until the period of the Maccabees and their successful expression of nationhood (c 160 B.C.), the psalms played a significant part in the life of the people.

The Hebrew title 'The Book of Praises' emphasises the spirit of thanksgiving and adoration found in the Psalter (116-118, 145-150). Yet there are many moods in the whole collection; joy, penitence, sadness, mourning, wonder, and national feeling are all in the wide range and variety of worship. For this reason, many today find inspiration and comfort in these age-old prayers and praises.

The Greek title word 'psalms' reminds us that a stringed instrument accompanied these songs. What was at first the name for a lyre became the name for the song that was sung. There are traditional musical directions at the heading of some of the psalms, although their meaning is obscure.

The whole collection from the third century B.C. was divided into five parts, perhaps recalling the five books of the Pentateuch at the beginning of the Bible (Ps 1-41; 42-72; 73-89; 90-106; 107-150).

Some psalms are like hymns. For example, Jubilate (100) has been translated into poetry (e.g. the hymn 'All people that on earth do dwell'). There are also Royal psalms, rejoicing at the kingship of God. Some of these have a flavour of expectancy, looking forward to the future coming of the Messiah (Ps 2, 20, 110). Many psalms express thanksgiving for God's protection through history (78, 107), others are meditations and instructions (119). The individual has found through the centuries strength and inspiration in psalms of trust (23), cries from the heart (130), utterances of penitence (51) and dirges of sorrow and depression (102).

The psalms interpret the nation's history. They also instruct the faithful in ways of prayer (42, 43). Some of them are 'cultic' and are used for ceremonies in connection with the formal worship of temple and synagogue (15, 136). Refrains and doxologies appear to indicate their use in corporate worship (e.g. at end of 41, 72, 89, 106). Scholars have done much to reveal the form of these psalms and to trace their sources.

Such collections as 'the song of ascents' (120-134) have a special character. Acrostic psalms (119, 145, 9-10, 25, 34, 37, 111, 112) have a distinctive form, perhaps to aid the memory, more probably to indicate the total response (the whole alphabet is in play) of words and praises in expressing the inexpressible.

The beauty and rhythm of the verses are haunting and colourful. 'Like as the hart ...', 'The Lord is my shepherd', 'My tongue is the pen of a ready writer.' No rhymes, but parallel verses, now affirming, now contrasting, sometimes intensifying, emphasise the theme, stir the imagination, and fortify the will.

The God of the psalms, the creator and sustainer of the universe, longs for the obedience of his creatures and demands from them holiness and penitence. He tempers justice with mercy. The psalmist at times curses the enemies and blasphemers (examples of these imprecatory psalms include 58; 68:21-23; 69:22-28; 109:5-19; 137:7-9) invoking divine vengeance (enemies are allegorised by some as 'sins').

There is little about life and death (16:10; 49:15; 'God will redeem my life; 73:24 'receive me into glory').

Christ's use of the Psalms (118:22; 82:6; 22:1; 31:5) has probably accounted for the opinion that the Psalter is among Christians 'the most widely read book of the Old Testament'.

PROVERBS

This collection of 'wisdom literature' is the earliest of the writings which personify Wisdom and picture her raising her voice in public (1:20) and warning the people. Scholars see the influence of Egypt, Canaan, and Mesopotamia in the thinking and mood of these colourful sign-posts to good behaviour. There are striking parallels to be found in the writings of Amenemopet, whose educational methods and principles were commissioned by the Pharaoh of that time in Egypt (1000 B.C.). Solomon, the traditional author of 3000 proverbs (1 Kgs 4:32), was a contemporary.

There is great uncertainty about the authorship of Proverbs. As is so often the case, they were probably compiled over a long period. While some of the collection may be Solomonic, it is clear that King Hezekiah's name (c. 716 B.C.) is linked with Proverbs, chapter 25. Other names are applied to further sections (Agur, 30:1-33; and Lemuel, 31:1-9).

The distinctive feature of Proverbs, as a guide for the young life and for discipline among families, is the emphasis laid upon 'the fear of the Lord as the beginning of wisdom' and 'the knowledge of God' as the source of understanding (9:10).

The words of counsel and prudence are addressed to the individual. Any reference to the nation or its history or its problems is remarkably absent.

Proverbs, like many of the Psalms, meditates on the law at a notably early stage in Israel's history.

The book falls into the following sections:

1. The prologue (1-9); wisdom built a house with seven pillars (9:1)
2. The proverbs of Solomon (10-22:16)
3. Sayings perhaps from Amenemopet (22:17-24:22)
4. The collection of Hezekiah (25-29)
5. The sayings of Agur (30:1-14) and Lemuel (31:1-9), two wise men from Arabia
6. The numerical or 'riddling' proverbs (30:15-33) have a special charm. 'Three things beyond my comprehension, four indeed that I do not understand: the way of an eagle … a snake … a ship in mid-ocean, the way of a man with a girl.'
7. The 'alphabetical' poem praises the ideal wife (31:10-31) in an appendix structured to aid the memory.

The whole book was probably written in its final form in the fifth century B.C. The New Testament includes fourteen quotations and some twenty further echoes from the Book of Proverbs (e.g. Mt 12:34: 'out of the abundance of the heart, the mouth speaks' (Prov 10:14); Lk 12:42 (Prov 31:15); Lk 14:28 (Prov 24:27); Lk 16:15 (Prov 21:2).

ECCLESIASTES

The writer is addressing a group which has assembled to think over the meaning of life and hopes for the future. He is a leader of thought, a preacher and also a teacher. The word in Hebrew behind the title *ecclesiastes* or 'the preacher' is *koheleth*. There is a call and a summons to a serious life implied in the name.

The message is not hopeful. There is realism in the opening declaration about life's meaninglessness. 'All is vanity'.

The 'son of David' is named as the author of these reflections (1:1). Ecclesiastes is one of the writings of the Wisdom literature that uses the association of Solomon with wisdom in its title. Ecclesiastes, however, is of a much later date and may be placed in the second half of the third century.

For all the pessimism in the discourse, there are also flashes of light and hopefulness. Some say these are editor's additions lest the readers become entirely fatalistic. Other scholars see in the contradictions clear evidence of the mind switching between hopefulness and despair.

The search is made for the better life. There is gloom about the future and all the uncertainties of Sheol and its vague intimation of immortality. Yet a distinction is drawn between theoretical and practical wisdom. A poor youth can be wiser than an influential old king (4:13). A living dog is better than a dead lion (9:4). A poor man by his wisdom once saved his small city in the face of a formidable attack; but as is wont to happen, no one remembered the poor man or realised that wisdom is better than strength (9:14-16).

The negative teaching can have the effect of spurring people into action. 'Cast your bread upon the waters' (11:1).

It is interesting to find that some of Ecclesiastes and its proverbial wisdom was used by the Qumran community and its way of life by the Dead Sea. (4 Q Koh is the reference in the Dead Sea Scrolls material.)

'There is a time for everything' (3:1) and 'a good name is better than precious ointment' (7:1). 'Truly the light is sweet' (11:7) and 'Remember your Creator' (12:1). Such shafts of radiance relieve the darkness. They appear to fill the vacuum of life's idle vanities.

Not unexpectedly, however, direct quotations from Ecclesiastes are scarcely to be found in the New Testament.

THE SONG OF SONGS

Its place in the Bible

The Song of Songs is counted among the Wisdom books. It is listed after Ecclesiastes in the English Bible and the name of Solomon is linked with it (1:1). Perhaps indeed some of the verses were sung in Solomon's day. The king's reputation for wisdom (1 Kgs 4:30, 32) was enhanced by his 3000 proverbs and 1005 songs. His name gave a continuing authority to many writings and compositions of much later date.

In the Hebrew Bible, the Song of Songs is the first of the five 'roll books' (*megilloth*). It, together with Ruth, Lamentations, Ecclesiastes, and Esther was read at festivals during the year. The Song of Songs, or 'the greatest Song', was appointed for Passover reading. It may seem strange that a book which makes no mention of God should be in the canon-list of the scriptures. Its inclusion emphasises the importance of Solomon's tradition.

Its theme

This song of love has been interpreted in various ways. It has been said that this is a book designed not to teach, but to celebrate. There is a strong note of joy in these lyrics which sing spontaneously of the mystery and delighted happiness of love. There is a special enthusiasm in the language and style. The colourful rose of Sharon, the lily of the valleys (perhaps rather 'the crocus') (2:1), and 'the anemone' are redolent of spring; the voice of the turtle dove, the gentle gazelle, and the beauty of hills and gardens lend colour and music to the songs.

The theme is love and can be interpreted in a number of ways – allegorical, literal, dramatic, or cultic.

The Jewish rabbis saw in these lyrics the relationship of Israel and God. The nation in other writings (e.g. Hosea) was seen as a bride in loving relationship with the Lord. The Christian writers in the early centuries of the church's history viewed the church as the Bride of Christ. The mystical writers found food for meditation as they pictured the individual's love for God.

CHAPTER 6

The Prophets

ISAIAH

Since the end of the eighteenth century, biblical scholars have concluded that while chapters 1-39 deal with the life and prophecy of Isaiah, the son of Amoz, in the eighth century B.C., the chapters 40-66 belong to a period some one hundred and fifty years later, at the end of the exile in Babylon.

The differences in the style of these two portions, the two distinct historical backgrounds, and the separate theological themes led J. C. Doederlein in 1775 to refer to 'the two Isaiahs'. It was noticed that as far back as 200 B.C., these 'two prophecies' had been put together in the four volumes of prophetic oracles described as 'Isaiah, Jeremiah, Ezekiel, and The Twelve'. It is interesting to note that in an earlier list of the Hebrew scriptures, Jeremiah and Ezekiel are both placed before Isaiah chapters 1-66; this gives some slight support to the claim that the latter portion of Isaiah was post-exilic.

Isaiah, chapters 1-39

The prophet's prominence in the nation's public affairs is impressive. He fulfils the role of politician, historian, and prophet.

As prophet, he is outstanding. In later days, he is referred to as *the* prophet *par excellence*. He points to God as the Holy One of Israel. He declares the justice and mercy and truth of God with a bold and courageous emphasis. Holiness is coupled with righteousness; it is quite different from the pietism that implies a withdrawal from life's activities, however turbulent they may be.

Earlier prophets were deeply concerned with social justice. Amos affirmed God's care for the poor; Hosea expounded love and human compassion in terms of personal relationships, physical suffering and the power of reconciliation. Isaiah includes their insights in his preaching and prophecy. His contemporary, the prophet Micah, appears also to influence this current thinking about people and their ordinary needs in life.

Isaiah's headquarters were apparently in the city of Jerusalem. We read of his public statements issuing from 'the middle court' (2 Kgs 20:4). Street-scenes colour his words; chariots, rich ladies, great houses, vineyards, and music-making come in for criticism. The prophet's words have weight as he seeks to disturb the consciences of the citizens and to remove their complacency. He speaks from a position of considerable authority, as a member of the royal family, having the ear of the king. His judgements, however, are not entirely negative. He also keeps alive among the people the hope that God promised to those who were faithful and obedient to his will and ways.

For some forty years, from King Uzziah's death in 740 B.C., the prophet was engaged in the kind of statesmanship which combined religious vision with a policy of government which was both practical and prudent. The nation was small in area, surrounded by great powers. Therefore, the quality of the life of the inhabitants, when frequently caught up in international issues not of their own making, became all-important. The following extract from Ecclesiasticus, chapter 48, written in or about the year 180 B.C. is illuminating:

> Hezekiah fortified his city,
> and brought water into the midst of it;
> he tunneled the sheer rock with iron
> and built pools for water.
> In his days Sennacherib [Assyrian king] came up,
> and sent the Rabshakeh [commander-in-chief)];
> he lifted up his hand against Zion
> and made great boasts in his arrogance.
> Then their hearts were shaken and their hands trembled,
> And they were in anguish, like women in travail,
> spreading forth their hands towards him;
> And the Holy One quickly heard from heaven
> and delivered them by the hand of Isaiah.
> The Lord smote the camp of the Assyrians,
> and his angel wiped them out.
> For Hezekiah did what was pleasing to the Lord.

And he held strongly to the ways of David, his father,
which Isaiah the prophet commanded,
who was great and faithful in his vision.
In his days the sun went backward,
And he lengthened the life of the king.
By the spirit of might he saw the last things
And comforted those who mourned in Zion.
He revealed what was to occur at the end of time,
And the hidden things before they came to pass.

Isaiah chapters 1-39 are not in chronological order. The subject takes precedence. Chapter 1 introduces the prophet's approach: if the people are obedient, 'ceasing to do evil and learning to do well', Zion will be redeemed with justice.

Only in chapter 6 do we read of Isaiah's call after his vision, described by R. Pfeiffer as 'the most revealing page he ever wrote'.

Chapters 13-23 form a collection of oracles. These are uttered against a number of foreign powers: Babylon, Moab, Damascus, Egypt, Tyre, among them.

There are five headings indicating the problems and events which drew forth messages and statements from Isaiah, conscious of his commission from the Lord.

(1) The atmosphere of idolatry and false religion needed to be cleared away with extreme urgency.

(2) The people heard uncomfortable words about Assyria. When the king, Tiglath-Pileser III (745-727 B.C.), invaded the Northern Kingdom, Assyria was declared to be 'the rod' of God's anger, an instrument of God's wrath, since the people had flouted God's laws. Their greed and injustices were punished by an outsider.

(3) When Sargon, who was king of Assyria from 722-705 B.C., captured the northern capital Samaria, and the deportation of the ten tribes followed, Isaiah sees in the event both judgement and hope. Important spiritual lessons would be learnt from such a disaster.

(4) Then a warning voice is sounded when Sargon clashes with Egypt. The temptation of putting trust in Egypt must be resisted.

Finally (5) at the unexpected, and perhaps never fully explained destruction of Sennacherib's army, the prophecies about a king, a very different kind of king with a Messianic charisma (11:1-9), restore confidence and foreshadow a triumph for righteousness and holiness. There is mention of a remnant; the nation, greatly reduced in numbers, will be seen to have a special role to play in world history. If those that are left are found faithful, they will never be a casual oddment of scattered survivors. The few will find a cohesion and a common purpose when entrusted with a mighty truth.

Isaiah 40-66

The style and language of these chapters have led scholars to the conclusion that this dramatic poem dates from a period long after Isaiah, in all probability after the exile was over and the return from Babylon to Jerusalem had been made. There is no mention of the prophet's name. Cyrus figures as the nation's deliverer from their plight as captives; from the year 555 B.C. he is in the ascendancy in the East. By the might of 'the Medes and the Persians', under the leadership of Cyrus, the fall of Babylon was accomplished (45).

There are three sections. They have been called 'cantos'. The language is beautiful; the poetry outstanding for its rhythm and the music of the words, both in the Hebrew and in many translations. Much of the tragedy and triumph of these chapters inspired the 'Messiah' of George Frederick Handel.

The first canto (40-48) sings of the futility and wickedness of idolatry; the second (49-55) paints the portrait of the Servant 'figure'; and the third, (56-66) praises God and gives him the glory for the return of the nation and the restoration of Zion.

1. Chapters 40-48 contain many words for the idols who come under the judgement of the prophet. The constant repetition of such phrases as 'fear not', 'do not be afraid', indicates the need for courage to break away from the influence of blind and dumb symbols of worship. Cyrus was used to solve a particular problem; deliverance in general, spiritual as well as military, is the nation's great need.

2. In the second canto, a deliverer emerges in the form of a Servant. This personality has a universal, not merely a local, purpose. Much scholarly discussion has been devoted to the whole subject of the servant-figure here described. The meaning

of his role in the drama is not fully clear. The Servant appears to be second only in importance to God himself. At first, he appears as a somewhat passive figure, the recipient of God's blessings and spiritual gifts. Then, in a more active role, he is depicted as representing not the whole nation, but that part of Israel which is faithful and responsive. Finally, he stands, in tragic isolation, a noble figure and yet intensely suffering. Here his Messianic commission points to a future age of blessedness and peace.

Isaiah 40-55: The argument of the Servant passages

The servant is calm and confident in a scene of crisis and confusion, since God is in control (41:8-20).

God's kingdom will come not by force or violence but through patient waiting and gentleness (42:1-9).

The nation, as Servant, has been blind and deaf in the past when God called (42:18-43:10).

Now they are promised that God has not forgotten them (44:1, 2, 21).

The servant is aware of his failure but God entrusts him with further responsibility (49:1-13).

The servant is found faithful but suffers in the process (50:4-9).

The servant is praised for his endurance and his example will carry far more weight than any words (52:13-end).

The onlookers are amazed (53:1-3). They begin to realise that the despised servant is suffering for their faults and folly (53:4-6). The servant suffered unjustly (53:7-9). This was God's plan: the servant gave himself as an offering for his people's sins that he might 'make many righteous' (53:10-12).

3. The third canto opens with a reminder of the need for righteous human action in the face of the coming of God's salvation (56:1-3). Then the joy of the return from exile comes to expression. Zion is bright with light (60:1-3). It is a spiritual centre for all sorts (60:4-9); from the East (verses 6 and 7) and from the West (verses 7-9). It is to be a Holy City (verse 14); a city of peace and no violence (verse 18). The walls will be called Salvation and the gates Praise (verse 18). The picture of a new heaven and a new earth (65:17) is painted in the language of vision and the poetry of apocalypse. Similar echoes of praise and future hope occur in the Revelation of St John the Divine, the New Testament's final book.

There are many quotations in the New Testament drawn from Isaiah 40-66 (for example, Mt 3:3; 8:17; 12:17-21; Lk 3:4-6, 4:17-19; Jn 1:23; 12:38; Acts 8:30-33; Rom 10:16). It is true that they are ascribed to Isaiah, but the chief point about them is that they are the words of scripture.

JEREMIAH

Jeremiah, the son of a priest, was probably not himself a priest, though a dedicated celibate in the service of God and the nation. Born c. 650 B.C. in Anathoth, near Jerusalem, in the stirring period of the seventh century, he served his country under five kings (Josiah, Jehoahaz, Jehoiakim, Jehoiachin, and Zedekiah). His call to serve (c. 627 B.C.) is vividly told; the prophet's humility is evident at once (Jer 1:4-10). He feels too young for the task, but he does not lack courage. His sense of responsibility is strong from the beginning and, a rare thing among his fellows at the time, he had a conscientiousness which was expressed in obedience to God and his laws.

Disobedience was the mood of the period. When Manasseh was king, there had been a retrogression after the partial reforms of his father, Hezekiah, whom he had succeeded around the year 695. The worship of 'the queen of heaven' (7:18), a Canaanite fertility-deity, was a challenge to young Jeremiah who swiftly gained a reputation for doom and gloom, although, in fact, his message when seen in perspective found hope at the end of the tunnel of disasters. There would be defeat and suffering at the hands of the two great nations, Egypt and Babylon, between which Judah was sandwiched. Yet there was hope to be found in unexpected quarters through the faithfulness of a remnant. The little group which escaped exile and remained in Judah was not to be that remnant; surprisingly, the faithful remnant, on whom hope for the future lay, was swept into exile and called to endure captivity between the years 597 and 538. Jeremiah communicated his message in many ways. His 'oracles' are powerful pieces of prophecy and judgement, containing hard messages from the Lord, as he maintained. There were also parables such as 'the two baskets of figs' (chapter 24) which brought out his point. The good figs (the exiled) would be instruments of God's loving care as well as his judgement.

Jeremiah felt happiest in the reign of Josiah (639-608), in whose time 'the book of the law' (possibly the book known to us as Deuteronomy) was found. The discovery astounded the king as he realised how far from the law his people had drifted. Josiah's reform in 621 B.C. was a highlight in this history which serves as a framework for the spiritual life and witness of the nation.

After Josiah, Jeremiah's voice sounds more trenchantly and the prophet has unpopular criticisms to make. There was a falling off in standards of worship and moral behaviour with the coming of Jehoiakim (607-597). The 'holiness' of God was obscured. The 'law' which had been discovered was not adequately practised; the people gave lip-service to its requirements and became complacent.

It seemed as if God was punishing the people through the might and tyranny of powerful empires such as Egypt and Babylonia. Matters came to a head with Nebuchadnezzar's attack on Jerusalem (597 B.C.). He carried away the people into captivity. The next king Jehoiachin, aged 18, with his mother, Nehushta, was also taken captive.

Jeremiah pointed out that the destruction of the Temple at the time of this invasion was a sign of God's judgement on the people who had thought that as long as they had 'the temple of the Lord' (chapter 7) in their midst, they need not make an effort to keep the covenant, to obey the law, or to pay attention to what the temple and its worship meant to the life of the individual and the nation.

The exile, on the surface a tragedy, need not be the end of the nation and certainly did not signify the failure of God. The exile itself could also be a sign of a change of heart and the preparation for another 'Exodus', a rescue from darkness and slavery for a new life.

Jeremiah has a distinctive message, not only for his own day but for the world, at any period. His 'jeremiad' is realistic, yet not entirely as pessimistic as it might appear to be, when he says 'the heart is deceitful and desperately wicked' (17:9). His target as prophet is just that: he works for a change of heart.

He also perceives that he is living in a new day. Sacrifices are not enough; covenants have to be re-enacted; Noah had a covenant, so had Abraham, so had Moses. In chapter 31:31 we read of a key passage in Jeremiah's teaching. A new covenant will be arranged; this will be a matter of the heart and a new spirit in a people, rescued not from Egypt as in the days of Moses, but from Babylon.

With such a message, Jeremiah could hardly escape suffering and confrontation with the authorities. Under King Zedekiah, (597) he faced threats to his life and imprisonment, with all the accompanying degradation (Jer 37-38).

The prophet himself did not go to Babylon. Nebuchadnezzar freed him from Zedekiah's authority when the second invasion in 587 took place. 'You can stay under Gedaliah the governor here in Judah' said the Babylonian king. (Chapter 39: 'They handed him over to Gedaliah to take him back to his home'.) However, in the end Jeremiah went to Egypt with other refugees and we presume that he died there.

Among the religious ideas found in the book of Jeremiah, the most important include the conviction that the 'just and right God' (9:24) is lord over other nations as well as Israel and the controller of history.

There is, however, a special relationship between Israel and God. This was just as much a responsibility as a privilege. Israel had not been faithful (2:13).

A new beginning was dawning and a new covenant envisaged (31:31-34). The relationship of the individual with God would be re-inforced. It is no surprise that Jeremiah uses the first person singular with great frequency, not only when he cries 'I do not know how to speak; I am only a child' (1:6) but on the many occasions when his head aches and his body is full of pain (9:1, 12:1, 15:18).

Jeremiah clearly loves his people and prays fervently both for friends and enemies. A lover of nature, too, he writes with great affection about his native land and its natural beauty. The loneliness of this warm personality is most moving; his humility (10:23) and his capacity for sacrifice (9:1; 31:16) are even more eloquent than his prophecies.

His writings have been classified as follows:

1.   1-25.   The judgement on the nation.

2.	26-36.	Oracles written in narrative form.
3.	37-45.	Jeremiah's life and ministry from the siege of Jerusalem until his days in Egypt.
4.	46-51.	Oracles against foreign nations.

Chapter 52 is an appendix similar to 2 Kings 24:18-25:30. Fragments of the Dead Sea Scrolls show that the book of Jeremiah existed in more than one form. The Greek Septuagint version also shows a different arrangement of the contents. This suggests that the book as we know it today received its final form at a relatively late date.

LAMENTATIONS

The Background

These sorrowful songs were clearly compiled after the fall of the city of Jerusalem in 587 B.C. Yet through the grief and gloom of the dirges and lamentations, sometimes called jeremiads, there shines a glimmer of hope pointing the way to a future (5:19-22).

Jerusalem in the years before its destruction had had a chequered history. The great powers of Egypt, Assyria, and now Babylon had been a constant threat. At intervals, however, especially during the reign of Josiah there had been a period of stability and somewhat uncertain peace. That king's reforms in 621 B.C. had brought new hopes, but these were dashed with the death of Josiah at the battle of Megiddo in 609. From that point, mounting trouble dogged the fortunes of Judah. No help was forthcoming from Egypt (4:17) to rescue the city from Nebuchadnezzar of Babylon. Little comfort was gained from Zedekiah's leadership as a vassal (4:20) after the first Babylonian attack and siege in 598. These slight historical references in Lamentations hint at the tragedy behind the sorrow. The suffering had been intense; the citizens were left leaderless; the temple, their spiritual centre, the symbol of their unity, was in ruins; the captivity, with exile in faraway Babylon, was a national and religious disaster.

The Message of Lamentations

In spite of these shattering experiences, the writers appear confident that God was still in control and had not deserted the people. There was a firm conviction that God had sent Babylon to discipline the disobedient and the rebellious in order that they might learn spiritual lessons in the hard way (1:17).

Those who were suffering would be obliged to wait. Their prayers would not be answered in any mechanical or predictable way (3:8, 44). They would discover that they benefited from 'bearing the yoke' while young (3:27).

Strangely, in this atmosphere of lament, new light is thrown upon hope for the future. Hope, however, must be seen as an activity, a way of life, and not merely a gift from above (3:22-27). God's love is 'new every morning'.

Authorship

Although Lamentations is placed after Jeremiah in the Latin and English versions, scholars consider that it is unlikely that the prophet was the author. The references to Egypt and Zedekiah would have been couched by him in less favourable language. The style of the writing in these five chapters of Lamentations points to the probability that many hands were involved in the compilation. Chapters 1, 2, 4, 5 have each 22 verses and their structure is based on the 22 letters of the Hebrew alphabet. Thus, the laments were easily memorised; their form had a distinctive dignity; and as pilgrim prayers they are recited annually in the late summer, according to Jewish custom, to commemorate the city's fall. In the Christian liturgy, echoes of Lamentations are heard during Holy Week when the passion and crucifixion are recalled. In Lamentations, Jerusalem is personified (1:9, 12); the city cries out, 'Look, O Lord, on my affliction – is it nothing to you, all you who pass by – is any suffering like my suffering?'

Summary

Lamentations opens with (1) a dirge-like mourning for the city's fall (1:1-11). This is followed by (2) an individual lament (1:12-22). (3) A lament of the whole community is added (3:40-45). Chapter 5, the so-called 'Prayer of Jeremiah', sings a psalm-like chant about 'the reversal of fortune', with sadness but without bitterness, looking ahead to the hoped-for return (5:21).

EZEKIEL

Even if each prophet is indebted to earlier prophets, and undoubtedly there is a touch of Amos in Ezekiel's utterance, there is at the same time much that is distinctive about this prophet of the exile.

Ezekiel, of a priestly family, is a visionary. He has a word from God both in Jerusalem and also by the waters of Babylon, the river Chebar.

In picturesque language, he describes his own calling at a time of his city's disasters: first, the initial attack on Jerusalem in 597 and the removal of the citizens to captivity and then again at the time of the city's destruction, Temple and all, in 587.

His opening vision, apocalyptic and packed with movement and weird imagery of bird, beast, and human life, makes him humbly aware of God's presence (chapters 1-3). The words that are given to him on a scroll, packed on both sides with an urgent message, Ezekiel eats. He, as a prophet, is himself a sign of God's action; he acts the parables he recounts. The word is the drama. His listeners believe the truth of what he says, even when Ezekiel himself is tongue-tied and struck speechless. The tile, the griddle, the sharp sword, the vision of the end, all illustrate that God punishes the people for their rebellion against him and their disobedience to the 'law of holiness' (Lev 19:2). Instead they are fatally attracted by Asherah, the fertility goddess of the Canaanites, on the one hand, and Tammuz, an Assyrian fertility deity.

The vigour of this prophet's denunciation is energetically sustained. The city is a stewpot and 'we are the meat' (11). What is needed by the citizens is a heart of flesh to replace a heart of stone.

The prophet emphasises the personal responsibility of each one who has sinned and rebelled. National leaders such as Nebuchadnezzar from Babylon and Psammetichus from Egypt are great eagles who swoop and punish (17). They are instruments of God, and the chosen people must not blame the past, with the slogan 'the fathers have eaten sour grapes and the children's teeth are set on edge'. To put it bluntly, 'the soul that sinneth, it shall die' (18).

Many cities and powers come in for denunciation: the two sisters, Oholah (Samaria) and Oholibah (Jerusalem), also Ammon, Moab, Eden, Philistia, Tyre (like a great ship), Egypt, Ethiopia (Cush) and Assyria (cedar tree).

After the fall of Jerusalem, the tone of Ezekiel's prophesying changes. He sounds the note of hope. 'I am for you' (36); he repeats that a heart of flesh must oust the heart of stone. A new Exodus (20) and a new covenant (16) must mark a new beginning for those that are left. The former shepherds (rulers) allowed the flock to be scattered (34). The dry bones which the visionary sees in the valley will put on flesh again and live: this chapter (37) is a highlight of the book.

The city is best left undefended 'without walls' (38:11 & Zech 2:4). The temple will be built again: the sacrifices will atone for the former destruction (sin-offering) and the apostasy and idolatry of the people (the guilt offering). The altar (of Babylonian architecture) will be built up, the Passover celebrated and streams of living water (47) up to the ankles, the knees, and the loins will refresh not only Israel, but a whole world.

DANIEL

The book of Daniel is the latest in date of the Old Testament writings. It is the first of the so-called 'apocalyptic writings' which belong to the period 200 B.C.-A.D. 100.

The word 'apocalyptic' suggests an unveiling of what is hidden and mysterious. The imagery and presentation is unlike the official prophetic style of writing. Yet there is prophecy within the mystery which is unfolded. Not only is the past interpreted but also the future is dimly, and often cryptically, outlined. 'Blessed is he who waits' (12:12) strikes an expectant note at the close of the book. The reader stands, as it were, on tip-toe with a vision of the end in view.

The book, which contains incidents and experiences from the days of Nebuchadnezzar, Belshazar his son, and Darius, King of the Medes and Persians (521-486 B.C.), was issued in its final form in the critical days of the second century B.C. Antiochus IV (175-163 B.C.), called 'Epiphanes or the Illustrious', was the archenemy of Israel. As King of Syria, he invaded Jerusalem and spread destruction. The temple was laid waste and desecrated

(168 B.C.). The abomination of desolation (11:31) sums up the horror of the sacrilege. If many were corrupted, with their faith violently damaged, there was a prophetic note in the assurance that 'the people who know their God shall stand firm and take action' (11:32). Before many years were to pass, the Maccabees would succeed in re-consecrating the sanctuary and restoring the daily sacrifice (164 B.C.).

The first six chapters give an account of the people of Israel dispersed among the powers of Babylon and then of Media and Persia.

Daniel's courage and bravery are recalled to restore confidence among the people. Dreams are interpreted and visions are dramatically described. The past is explained in picturesque story-telling. Daniel understood all the visions and dreams (1:17). In this section occurs Nebuchadnezzar's dream of the great image 'mighty and of exceeding brightness' (2:31). Another dream of a tree with its branches cut and only the stump left (4:13,14) is interpreted by Daniel. The 'writing on the wall' is also deciphered by him; he explains the terse Aramaic sentence which prophesies ominously 'counting, weighing, and dividing' (5:25).

These incidents are more than traditional tales of wonder and mystery. They are recorded to illustrate the strong faith, fortified by the wisdom, prayer, and remarkable courage, that shines through the narrative. Daniel's prayer, three times a day, linked with the worship in far-away Jerusalem is exemplary (6:10). The fiery furnace and the den of lions illustrate the victory, not the overthrow, of faith in the one true God.

Chapter 7 links together the first and second parts of the book. Daniel's vision of one 'like a son of man' after the haunting dream of four beasts has had several interpretations (7:13). No one is clear about who this 'human figure' is meant to be, similar perhaps to an angel but perhaps conveying a hint of a future Messiah.

In chapters 8-12, Daniel finds himself puzzled by his own dreams. He, who interpreted so clearly the dreams and visions of great leaders, is baffled by his own experiences. He was humbled by his failure to understand them: 'He was overcome and lay sick for some days – appalled' (8:27).

In the end, Daniel 'the man greatly beloved' (10:11) received re-
assuring answers to his prayers. Although there would be a time
of 'wrath' (11:44) and violence, faithfulness and hope are the important things to sustain. The people are not able to bring in a
kingdom, but their hope in God's rule convinces them that they
need not depend on world events. Chapter 11 traces the course
of history through the preceding centuries. There are veiled references to Nebuchadnezzar of Babylon (605-562 B.C.) and his
son Sheshbazzar, and also to Darius of Persia (521-486 B.C.) and
Alexander the Great (died 323 B.C.). Egypt and Syria, 'the kings
of South and North' (11:5, 6) threaten, but even Antiochus IV
(175–163 B.C.), the fiercest of the Seleucid dynasty from Syria,
did not succeed in imposing his pagan culture on the Israel he so
violently attacked.

The book of Daniel is associated with three languages: Chapters
1 and 8-12 are in Hebrew; chapters 2-7 in Aramaic (the language
used by Israel in Persian affairs as in Ezra 4:7); there are addi-
tional portions of Daniel in Greek; these are included in the
Apocrypha as Susanna, Bel and the Dragon, and the Song of the
Three Children. The Hebrew Bible places Daniel among the
Writings and not with the Prophets, although there is much
prophecy amid the apocalyptic.

HOSEA

Hosea has been called 'the prophet of Israel's decline and fall'
(Cheyne). He lived in a very dark period of the history of the
northern kingdom of Israel. The situation deteriorated rapidly
from the death of Jeroboam II in 743 B.C. Both Hosea and Amos
prophesied in the northern kingdom during the eighth century.

Hosea, unlike Amos, prophesied in his own country, Israel.
Amos, from the southern kingdom Judah, had been an outsider;
he had been forcibly struck by the extremes of wealth and
poverty that he found when he arrived. Hosea, a younger contemporary, knew more intimately the causes of his country's
failures and weaknesses. He loved his own people but was
deeply disappointed in them. Their religious life was marked by
faithlessness. They deserted the Lord for Baal. They were blind
and 'lacked knowledge' (4:6). The priests were of no help: 'like
people, like priest' cried the prophet (4:9) meaning that the leaders were no wiser than the people who had been entrusted to
their leadership.

This unreliability Hosea compares with the faithlessness in his own home. He writes out of the bitter experience of his broken family life and knows how much damage to human relationships results. Gomer, his wife, however, is restored to partnership with Hosea and abandons her lover (3). There is a lesson for the whole country in this reconciliation. Hosea's willingness to receive his wife back again is an example from a real life situation of God's readiness to be merciful to the wayward people who have strayed from his laws. God loves the people in spite of everything. He desires steadfast love above all else (6:6).

The political situation is clearly critical. It is not certain if Hosea actually lived to see Samaria under siege in 722 B.C. (10:7, 15), but he foresaw the foolishness of 'Ephraim'; like 'a silly dove' the nation thought that there was a hopeful future in an alliance with Egypt. 'Ephraim is a cake not turned' (7:8). In these vivid words, the one-sided policy of the country involved enmity with another power, such as Assyria (7:11). The policies are empty or else ill-founded: 'they sow the wind and they shall reap the whirlwind' (8:7). 'Ephraim has hired lovers' (8:9). They will feel deep despair: 'They shall say to the mountains, Cover us; and to the hills, Fall on us' (10:8).

There is a need for righteousness to be re-established. This involves hard work. 'Break up your fallow ground' (10:12). God longs for his people to be with him; he loves them as always: 'when Israel was a child, then I loved him and called my son out of Egypt'. The Exodus is never quite forgotten (11:1). God disciplines; it is an expression of his love. Hosea uses picture-words from a ploughing scene when he writes, 'I drew them with cords of a man, with bands of love' (11:4). After punishment at the hands of Assyria, there will be a return. God promises 'I will redeem them from death: O death, where are thy plagues? O grave, where is thy destruction?' (13:14).

Penitence is the solution of the national problem, not animal sacrifice: 'We will render as bullocks the offering of our lips' (14:2).

The closing words of the book echo Psalm 107:43: 'Who is wise, he shall understand these things – the ways of the Lord are right' (14:9).

JOEL

Although the book of Joel is placed between the books of Hosea and Amos in the biblical order, the date of this writing is much later. It is more probably from the period of the second temple and might be dated in the first half of the fifth century between the revival of worship described by Haggai and the religious reforms of Ezra.

There are echoes of Amos (Amos 1:8-12) in chapter 3; Tyre, Edom and Philistia are all under judgement. Joel, however, appears much more as a document written in a finished, literary style rather than a rhetorical prophecy delivered to a live audience.

It has been thought that it was composed for a great festival, perhaps the Feast of the Ingathering or a harvest thanksgiving in the autumn (Ex 23:16). The prophecy is suitable both for reading and also for liturgical use. The Christians chose it for reading in the season of Lent. The references to repentance, 'rend your hearts and not your garments' (2:13), and to fasting, (2:15), are vigorous and spiritually searching.

Joel is one of those prophets who speaks to our human condition, whatever the period. He is the one who tells of 'old men dreaming dreams and young men seeing visions' (2:28). There is a lively spirit in his frequently quoted phrase, 'Fear not, o land'. He writes reassuringly (2:21). The Lord 'will restore the years that the locusts have eaten' (2:25). This good news follows a highly dramatic account of the devastation that an army of locusts can bring; the devouring fire, the burning flames, the rumbling of chariots and the crackling of flames consuming the stubble are powerfully described (2).

The truths may be unpalatable with naught for the people's comfort. Yet if there is a change of heart, a heart-break more drastic than the tearing of garments, the prophet promises hope and an outpouring of God's spirit (2:28).

The positive message of Joel has special point for those who have returned to their own land and are able to harvest its fruits (2:26). Furthermore, the worship of God and his presence among the people give assurance that they will 'never again be put to shame' (2:27). The Lord is near them to give protection 'in the valley of decision' (3:14). The last words depict God active in

history: 'The Lord dwells in Zion'. Egypt and Edom no longer
threaten (3:19-21).

AMOS

The date of the call of Amos has been thought to be around 750
B.C. Subsequently the Assyrians attacked Samaria. Then came
the carrying away of captives in 730 B.C. The siege and destruction of the city in 722 B.C. followed.

Although there had been prophets, such as Nathan and Elijah, in
the nation's history, the book of Amos is the earliest detailed
written prophecy.

In its message, a deep concern for social justice is expressed in
powerful language. In a period of comparative peace and prosperity, the few were affluent, but the numerous poor were oppressed and underprivileged. A time of luxury was a time of
temptation and greed. God's law was largely forgotten. The
prophet had important things to say about God's judgement in
history. A 'day of the Lord' was prophesied. So far from being
the dawn of a golden age, this 'day' would be a moment of justice and humiliation.

Amos was not a professionally trained prophet. Living at a time
when there were two kingdoms, Judah and Israel, he was called
to build bridges. A native of Tekoa in Judah, this keeper of sheep
found himself in Israel, the northern kingdom, as an outsider
and a bearer of uncomfortable tidings.

Jeroboam II was the King of Israel and Uzziah was King of Judah.
Both kingdoms as well as the nations in the neighbourhood surrounding them receive stern, unpalatable news. Syria suffers
and its people go into captivity; Philistia is destroyed; Tyre is
burnt, as are Edom, Ammon and Moab. Judah too will have to
face destruction because it has rejected 'the law of the Lord'
(2:4). Israel's corruption consists in selling 'the righteous for sil-
ver, and the needy for a pair of shoes' (2:6).

Israel flouted the law of God and ungratefully forgot that they
had been rescued from the Amorite, one of the Canaanite enemies (2:9). God had rescued them from Egypt and made those
who were Nazirites specially dedicated to the service of God.
Now Israel wanted to do away with them. The prophets also
were ordered not to prophesy (2:12).

Amos, the shepherd, speaks forcibly, with rustic language. He has little use for the kind of worship which is not followed up with righteous acts. The enemies of Israel, such as Egypt and Assyria, will descend upon those who are living a life of ease and luxury. A few only will be rescued, says the shepherd-prophet, 'as the shepherd rescues out of the mouth of the lion two legs, or a piece of an ear' (3:12).

The prophet speaks ironically about their worship. He foretells famine, drought, pestilence. He sees them as 'a brand plucked out of the burning' (4:11). 'Prepare to meet thy God, O Israel', he cries out (4:12). 'Seek good, and not evil, that ye may live' (5:14).

Then, significantly, Amos speaks of 'the day of the Lord'. This is the first mention of the great popular hope that God will give Israel victory over her enemies. Amos describes it as a day of darkness and not of light (5:18) because of the mockery which they have made of worship, and their laziness, and self-indulgence, their ivory beds and bowls of wine (6:4, 6). The city will be delivered up.

Amos emphasises the message of woe with illustrations of devouring locusts and raging fire. He sees in a vision 'a plumb-line' (7:7) and 'a basket of summer fruit' (8:2).

A violent earthquake is prophesied (9:1) but in the end there will be a restoration (9:11), ruins will be repaired; those who were in captivity will be re-instated.

OBADIAH

This is the shortest book in the Bible. The prophet has a vision of the destruction of Edom, the arch-enemy of Israel for many generations.

The reference to Esau (verse 9) recalls the rivalry with Jacob. Rebekah, their mother, had a premonition of this before they were born: 'Two nations are in your womb and two peoples from within you will be separated; one people will be stronger than the other, and the older will serve the younger' (Gen 25:22, 23).

The date of the book in its final form is apparently from the time of the capture of Jerusalem in 586 B.C. (verses 10 and 11). Edom's part in the city's downfall is vehemently denounced in

Psalm 137:7 ('Down with it, down with it, even to the ground' the Edomites had said and their words would not be forgotten). See also Ezek 35:15 and Lam 4:21.

The similarity between the opening words of Obadiah's vision (verses 1 and 2) and Jeremiah's prophecy 'concerning Edom' (Jer 49:7-22) raises the question of a possible independent source, used by both prophets. It may be that Obadiah influenced Jeremiah, or vice-versa.

Obadiah emphasises the exclusiveness of Israel among her neighbours. Edom ultimately became merged into Arabia Petraea after the fall of Jerusalem in A.D. 70. The reference to the rock (verse 3) and its clefts is a reminder of the grandeur and inaccessibility of Edom's mountains, in the midst of which lay Petra, the 'rose-red city, half as old as time'.

JONAH

The book of Jonah is a story rather than a prophecy. It has a missionary message, for the challenge given to Jonah involves a journey out and beyond the nation's boundaries. At first, he refuses to take it up and, when he changes his mind and preaches repentance to the inhabitants of Nineveh as he has been commissioned to do, he complains about his own success. Nineveh did repent and received many blessings and benefits.

Jonah the son of Amittai is mentioned in 2 Kings 14:25 and lived in the reign of Jeroboam II (786-746 B.C.) The book is anonymous and does not claim to be by Jonah. Indeed the language of this story, with echoes of Jeremiah and Ezekiel, indicate that it was written after the exile, perhaps in the fifth century.

Narrow racialism is rejected. In this, the book has a certain affinity with the Book of Ruth. Israel is taught about the merciful loving-kindness of God by the penitence and sincere humility of a city which has been an enemy capital. The 'sign of Jonah' referred to in the New Testament (Mt 12:39-41 and Lk 11:29–32) helps home the teaching of Jesus about the universality of God's love and, albeit obscurely, his power to give life.

The *de profundis* note (2:3) and Jonah as a symbol of misfortune (1:12) add a dramatic touch to this parable. Both the sea and Nineveh were symbols of hostility. The storm, the fish and the gourd indicate God's control.

Some see in this cheerful narrative, with sailors, king, people and the animals ('also much cattle') all in happy mood, a fresh outlook, less narrow, more generous, as God extends his forgiveness widely and promptly. Jonah himself was taken aback by it all and had to be reassured with a separate sign of divine power. Nineveh, of course, had been in ruins since 612 B.C. but probably continued to symbolise a menacing power and a typical enemy, which threatened the nation from outside. Is it possible that the contrast of Jonah's universalism and the strict conservatism of Ezra both pointed to the tensions involved in observing the faith in its wholeness in those days?

MICAH

Micah was apparently the youngest of the four eighth-century prophets, with Amos, Hosea and Isaiah. Like Isaiah, he came from Judah, while Amos and Hosea worked in the northern kingdom.

Micah's home was in the midst of farming country, in the Shephelah, the maritime plan in south-west Judah, some twenty-five miles from Jerusalem. He was of peasant stock.

Serving during the reigns of Jotham, Ahaz and Hezekiah in the period before the fall of Samaria (721 B.C.), he pointed critically at the moral and social wrongs committed by the wealthy at that time. The capitalist, the usurer, the swindler as well as the corrupt judges and the grasping priests became his target as he prophesied. He had scarcely the standing to influence political life in the manner of an Isaiah. He is more like an Amos in his concern for the small farmers who were at the mercy of invading armies and for the deprivations suffered by the villagers.

Micah foretold the destruction of Jerusalem. 'Zion shall be plowed as a field', he prophesied (3:12). This was a prophecy which may have saved Jeremiah's life a hundred years later. (Jer 26:18).

Many consider that Micah was a strong influence in the steps taken by King Hezekiah for religious reform. His preaching on repentance was as powerful as Isaiah's. He also looked ahead through the shadows to the promise of a new age, in famous words: 'Thou, Bethlehem Ephrathah, which art little to be among the thousands of Judah, out of thee shall one come forth to me that is to be ruler in Israel' (5:2).

Micah is renowned for his protest against formalism in religion. His style of writing, full of passion and righteous indignation, is at times obscure. There is nothing ambiguous, however, about the oft-quoted words that reveal the courage and zeal of this prophet, when he asks, 'What does the Lord require of you but to do justice and to love kindness and to walk humbly with your God?' (6:8).

There is much scholarly discussion about the unity of the book. It is thought that chapters 1-3 are certainly to be dated in eighth century, while the rest of the book may have been a collection of sayings and prophecies arranged in their final form at a much later date.

There are four parts in this prophecy:

1.	1:2-3:12	The denunciations of Israel.
2.	4:1-5:15	The promises made to Zion.
3.	6:1-7:7	Israel rebuked again.
4.	7:8-20	Hopes for restoration and 'the building of the walls'.

NAHUM

Little is known with any certainty about Nahum, whose name suggests 'comfort' or 'compassion'.

The author wrote his vision in a book. The subject deals mainly with the fall of Nineveh, the Assyrian capital, in 612 B.C. There are traces of liturgical writing in the text: chapter 1:2-10 is an acrostic poem: some 15 letters of the Hebrew alphabet introduce the verses in turn, although there is some disarray in the ordering.

The poetry of chapters 2 and 3 is among the finest in biblical literature. It is difficult to know if Nahum is predicting Nineveh's overthrow or writing during or after the event. The imperfect tense of Hebrew verbs may be either present or future!

There is no condemnation of Israel. This oracle or prophecy is spoken against a nation which has been under God's judgement. Assyria had on occasion been seen as an instrument of God's wrath upon the disobedient people of Israel (Is 10:5: 'Assyria, the rod of mine anger'). Nahum writes of Assyria's overthrow by the Babylonians and the Medes. This defeat is recorded in The Babylonian Chronicle (British Museum 21901, 38–50):

'Kyaxares (the Median king) made the King of Babylonia to cross and march along the Tigris river bank and pitch camp by Nineveh. They made a strong attack – city was taken – a great defeat – Sin-shar-ishkun, the Assyrian king, (perished in the flames)'. (Nahum 3:18).

There had been great names in the history of the mighty Assyrian empire from as early as 2000-1500 B.C. Nineveh had been the residence of Sennacherib (705-681 B.C.), Esar-haddon (680-668 B.C.) and Ashurbanipal (668-626). The lion (Nahum 2:11) had symbolised the strength of their armies.

HABAKKUK

There is great uncertainty about the historical background of this book. The prophet appears to be writing about the reign of a king whose rule has been far from satisfactory. Some suggest Manasseh (687-641) or Amon (641-639); others incline to place the setting in Jehoiakim's reign (609-597 B.C.).

A key phrase expresses the prophet's confidence as he converses with the Lord: 'The just shall live by his faith' (2:4). This sentence probably means that trustworthiness and faithful observance of the law will prevail in spite of the sense of hopelessness and even scepticism, expressed in 1:2: 'How long shall I cry for help and thou wilt not hear?' In New Testament times, St Paul expounded 'the just living by faith' out of his own experience. Later still, Martin Luther found these words crucial.

Of particular interest is the commentary on the first two chapters discovered in the scrolls at Qumran. The reference (1:6) to the 'bitter and hasty' nation is interpreted not as 'Chaldeans' but 'Kittim' meaning Greeks of the Seleucid dynasty or perhaps the invading Romans in the later period.

Chapter 3, separate from the prophecy, is a prayer in the form of a psalm, praising God for delivering his people. This may have been sung at the autumn festival when the covenant made by God with his people was renewed. Paran (3:3) recalls the law-giving on Mount Sinai.

ZEPHANIAH

Zephaniah's prophecy, traditional in its warnings against coming doom, impressive for its trenchant poetry (1:15) may have been designed for liturgical use in the temple in the period leading up to the reforms of King Josiah.

There is language here to discourage vehemently the following of Baal and Molech. The Lord will rescue a remnant and a great day of decision and judgement approaches. The temple worship must be true and just, universal not localised.

Powerful is the prophecy that the Lord will make a clean sweep (1:2) and take the initiative among the mighty nations. The 'sweeping' may recall the autumn Festival of the Ingathering with vigorous overtones for the city of Jerusalem which sorely needs renewal.

Jerusalem is not named as the city in chapter 3 but the point would be taken by its citizens. There was too much oppression of the people; those in charge of civic administration are vividly described as 'wolves of the evening' (3:3). They come out, darkly, under cover of night, to scavenge and plunder. Pride in their own achievements is their root sin.

Zephaniah's note of hope, after his realistic warning of correction and change, gives new heart to the small number surviving the days of turbulence and disaster. 'I will gather you, at that time I will bring you home' says the Lord (3:20). This closing song of Zephaniah's prophecy becomes a celebration, an act of worship, an affirmation of trust in Yahweh, be the times never so bitter and uncertain.

HAGGAI

This prophet apparently remembered the former glory of the old Temple (2:3). He may have come from Babylon back to Jerusalem with Zechariah and Zerubbabel.

The prophecy is almost entirely concerned with the rebuilding of the Temple. There is very careful dating (1:1, 15; 2:1, 10, 20). A sense of urgency is felt, with quick decisions made and the rapid progress of events. Ezra (6:15) writes of the completion of the temple in the sixth year of Darius.

Haggai gives his message to the people (later called 'the remnant') as well as to Zerubbabel the governor and Joshua the high priest. The people are referred to as the remnant: they are not simply survivors left over after the end of the captivity, but they have a function. With them rests the ushering in of the 'new age' and the part which they may be called upon to play at a critical time. The shaking of the nations (2:7) and the overturning of royal thrones (2:22) are powerful phrases used by the prophet who points to the wider significance of events. The closing words which give divine authority to the governor are striking: 'I will make you like my signet ring, for I have chosen you, declares the Lord.' The remnant also inherits the past blessings given to the nation.

The people had been slow to build the temple. They were ready enough to look after their own houses, panelled ones at that (1:4). Small wonder that there had been a famine. The people expected too much on their return: 'What you brought home, I blew away' saith the Lord' (1:9). There was no roof on the Temple. The work was important not for selfish reasons but because proper honour must be paid to the glory of God.

There had been a seventy-year interval since the destruction of the Temple. Not many would have remembered. There would have been glowing reports of its grandeur. However, the prophet assures them that the latter glory will be greater than the former glory (2:9). God's presence among them will be more fully appreciated after the destruction and suffering.

'There is a dead thing among them' (Barnes), that is to say the ruined temple, so the people are defiled (2:14) or this may be a reference (cf Ezra 4:1-5) to the quarrel arising from Zerubbabel's refusal to allow the people of Samaria to have a share in the rebuilding. Ezra (6:14) mentions the preaching of Haggai and Zechariah while the building work was reaching completion.

ZECHARIAH

It is generally agreed that this book falls into two sections: chapters 1-8 and 9-14. Indeed Zechariah's name does not appear in the collection of oracles which forms the second section.

Chapters 1-8 are from the pen of Zechariah. We learn from Ezra (Ezra 5:1 and 6:14) that both Zechariah and Haggai were concerned to encourage the completion of the Temple. Their preaching and prophecy played a successful part in this important project.

The date of this first part of Zechariah is around 519 B.C., 'in the eighth month of the second year of Darius' who was the Persian king from 521-486 B.C. The exiled people of Israel had already returned but much work on the Temple needed to be undertaken in order to follow up the building achievement of Nehemiah. The return to Jerusalem is an historical event with moral and ethical overtones: it is a time for the people to 'turn from evil ways and evil deeds' (1:4).

Zechariah, in a series of no fewer than eight visions, prophesies about the Temple and the choosing of Jerusalem (3:2).

These visions have been described as prophetic rather than apocalyptic, although some of the colourful imagery is found in both literary genres. Zechariah uses his vivid illustrations to reinforce the message of his preaching:

(1) The horsemen patrol the earth (1:10). There is peace and an opportunity to gain security for Jerusalem (1:7-17).

(2) The four horns, strong forces hostile to Jerusalem, are broken by four smiths. The site is prepared (1:18-21).

(3) The man with the measuring-line designs Jerusalem as an open city 'without walls' (2:4), a city with a great future: 'Many nations shall join themselves to the Lord in that day and shall be my people'.

(4) The vision of Joshua the high priest, 'a brand plucked from the burning' (3:2), a phrase already used by Amos (Amos 4:11). Joshua is purified, 'his filthy garments' are removed (3:4) and new robes of office give him authority over the Lord's 'house and his courts' (3:7). 'My servant, the Branch, is mentioned at this point: perhaps this refers to Zerubbabel, the city's governor, or else to a hint of a future Messiah.

(5) The lampstand with seven lamps indicate 'the seven eyes of the Lord which range over the whole earth' (4:10), the all-seeing, all-knowing God who has urged that the work will be accomplished 'not by might, nor by power, but by my Spirit' (4:6). The two olive trees, one on the right and the other on the left, may represent the two 'anointed with oil', the High Priest and the princely Messiah.

(6) The flying scroll will punish thieves and all evil-doers (5:1-4).

(7) The woman in a measuring-basket, or *ephah*, symbolises 'wickedness' (5:7). She is sent far away to Babylon, 'the land of Shinar' (5:11).

(8) The four chariots are the four winds (6:5). They patrol the earth (6:7).

The outlook for the future is promising, but with the prosperity there are responsibilities to be undertaken by the people. Zechariah has a warning (7:8): 'Thus says the Lord, render true judgement, show kindness and mercy each to his brother, do not oppress the widow, the fatherless, the alien or the poor'. Fasting is not enough, righteousness is required. Then (8:22) many peoples and strong nations will come to seek the Lord of hosts. 'In those days ten men from the nations of every tongue shall take hold of the robe of a Jew, saying, 'Let us go with you, for we have heard that God is with you'.

In the second section, there is no mention either of Darius or of Zechariah. This collection of oracles has phrases similar to the language of Malachi. The vision of the day of the Lord, 'your king comes to you' (9:9), shines through scenes of strife among enemies, including Greece (9:13). These prophecies may be associated with the fight for freedom in which the Maccabees were engaged (c 168-161 B.C.).

MALACHI

This prophecy may have been written shortly before Nehemiah's return to Jerusalem in 444 B.C. Malachi 'my messenger' (3:1) refers to the reluctance to pay tithes, the slackness of the priests who found their sacrificial duties burdensome (1:13). These and other problems were faced and dealt with by Nehemiah when he came.

The six sections into which the book may be divided are introduced with discussion, dispute, and leading questions. There is a sense of drama in these prophecies, applied as they are to current problems.

The dialogue between the Lord, whose words are spoken by the prophet, and the people aims at clearing up misunderstandings. For example, 'you have said harsh things against me' says the Lord. 'Yet you ask, what have we said against you?' You have said 'it is futile to serve God – what did we gain? – the evil doers prosper.' The answer comes from the Almighty: 'I will spare them, just as in compassion a man spares his son' (3:13ff).

The subjects of these six sections are not obvious. Yet for all their obscurity they point to an answer.

First (1:1-5), believe it or not, 'the Lord loves Jacob' and this is emphasised by the apparently continuing rejection of Esau with dire results for Edom territory.

Second (1:6-2:9), the standards of priesthood have so much deteriorated that God is dishonoured. The description of priesthood in the old Levite tradition illustrates what a priest can do for a people (2:5): 'My covenant was with him' says the Lord, 'a covenant of life and peace – he revered me – the lips of a priest … to preserve knowledge, and from his mouth men should seek instruction – because he is the messenger (Malachi) of the Lord'.

The third section likens Judah's faithlessness towards God to marital infidelity (2:10-16).

Fourth, the charge against God's injustice is met by a heavy warning about the Lord's coming with stern and cleansing judgement (2:17-3:5).

Fifth, it becomes clear that non-payment of tithes is equivalent to robbing God (3:6-12). Finally, when 'the great and terrible day of the Lord comes' (4:5), the righteous will understand the distinction between the righteous and the wicked. 'They will be mine' (3:17).

CHAPTER 7

Apocrypha

There are fifteen titles in the collection of books printed between the books of the Old Testament and those of the New in a number of editions of the Bible. These 'apocryphal' books provide valuable evidence for the study of developments in devotional, liturgical, and apocalyptic thinking during the 'intertestamental period' covering the second and third centuries B.C.

The name 'Apocrypha' or 'hidden writings' dates from the time of Jerome (A.D. 342-420), the translator of the Latin Vulgate version of the scriptures. He separated the apocryphal books from the regular canonical list of authoritative writings. The apocryphal books appear to have been 'half-in and half-out' of the Christian scriptures. They are not in the Hebrew scriptures.

The Council of Trent (1546) declared that they were canonical. The word 'deutero-canonical' was applied to them by certain other traditions; they were, so to speak, counted as 'border-line', valuable for their spiritual content but not important for the establishing of authoritative doctrine.

The first book of Esdras (1 Esdras) is closely connected with the Old Testament and contains passages taken from Ezra, part of Nehemiah, and 2 Chronicles. The story of the three young men at the banquet of King Darius occurs in chapter 3: 'Let us state what one thing is strongest,' they say. One of them, Zerubbabel, declares that 'Great is truth, and strongest of all', stronger than wine, the king, or women.

2 Esdras attempts in the language of apocalypse to reconcile God's goodness, justice, power and wisdom with the world's evils. Tobit, a moral tale, written with great charm, illustrates God's faithful care for those who serve him faithfully. Judith's part in saving the nation from Nebuchadnezzar's invasion is

grimly told. She decapitates the enemy's commander-in-chief, Holofernes. The details are horrific (13). The six additions to the Book of Esther supplement the Esther of the Old Testament, adding references to God which are strikingly absent in the latter. The Book of Wisdom, dating from the end of the first century B.C., is quoted in St Paul's epistles (e.g. Rom 9:21-23; Eph 6:11-17). Its blending of Jewish religion and Greek philosophy had considerable influence on early Christian thought. Ecclesiasticus is a book of instruction written by one Jesus, son of Sirach (50:27). It was translated from the original Hebrew into Greek by his grandson in 132 B.C., as stated in the prologue. The chapters which honour the physician (38) and praise famous men (44) have a special dignity. Baruch and the Letter of Jeremiah are, like Lamentations, appendices to the book of Jeremiah. Baruch was the prophet's secretary. The Song of the Three Young Men, Susanna, and Bel and the dragon, are additions to Daniel. 1 Maccabees contains a history of the Jews from the accession of Antiochus Epiphanes (175 B.C.) to the death of Simon Maccabaeus in 135 B.C. 2 Maccabees deals with the Maccabean wars ending with the victory of Judas Maccabaeus in 161 B.C. Both books recount the stirring story of the Jewish minority struggling against the Syrian powers.

It is interesting to note that when the Revised Standard Version of the Oxford annotated Apocrypha appeared in 1977 and was bound up with the Bible, the co-editor observed 'this expanded version is the only edition of the Bible in English that contains all the books regarded as authoritative by all branches of the Christian Church, including the several Eastern Orthodox Churches, and provides for the first time the complete canon of their Sacred Scriptures. The story of the making of the Revised Standard Version of the Bible is an account of the slow but steady triumph of ecumenical concern over more limited sectarian interests'.

In these days, when dialogue between Christians and Jews is in progress, much common ground, both spiritual and religious, is found by them through their study of the scriptures. Christians have been paying increasing attention to the Old Testament, where the roots and origins of their faith lie. This makes possible a fuller understanding of the scriptures and a clearer perception of what 'the Law and the Prophets' mean in the Jewish Church.

PART II

The New Testament

CHAPTER 8

Introduction

The New Testament continues the story of a people chosen by God. Yet particular attention is focused upon a person, born among that people, with a destiny, not only new but unique. All is now concentrated on Jesus Christ and the new life brought to those who followed him and believed in him. They belonged to the Body of Christ and membership was not confined to one nation. Israel, its history and heritage, were not forgotten, but those living the life of faith in Christ and obedience to him were to be called the New Israel. Jesus himself was pictured as a New Moses with a fresh approach to the law and a new commandment to give.

The New Testament announces good news; it has a gospel to proclaim. There is little formal philosophy in its writings. There are few reflections upon heaven and earth in general terms. Little about life beyond death is to be found in its teachings. On the other hand, events which took place when Herod was king and Pontius Pilate was the Roman imperial governor are counted as of supreme significance. The birth, sufferings, death, resurrection and exaltation of Jesus Christ make news which is still alive and fresh. Soon in the development of the Christian Church, creeds were formulated. These same events were frequently retold and known by heart. Their meaning was expounded. 'Dogma', when formulated, was not deadly and dry, but rather was found to be living truth, based on factual evidence, and an expression of a powerful, even revolutionary, faith.

The earliest writings of the New Testament are the epistles of Paul the Apostle and others. The word 'epistle' simply means 'letter' (from the Greek word *epistolé*). These letters, usually composed by an individual writer, were addressed to various groups of the faithful in different places. For the most part, they appear to have been written for people who were familiar with the Christian message. The problems which they faced are dealt with in these letters; in this way the deeper meaning of the person and message of Jesus is brought out and can be seen to influence every side of human life, both private and public. These letters are written in particular situations and so it is important to examine their background and context.

The two letters to the Galatians and the Romans, for example, both expound in different ways the meaning of Law in life: they handle the doctrine of justification by faith in Jesus Christ for the benefit of those who found attractive the old customs and ways of Judaism.

The first letter to the Corinthians contains much discussion about the typical problems and temptations of a life in a cosmopolitan city. The famous chapter on love (1 Cor:13) stands out brilliantly among the arguments and disputes to give a new vision of life's beauty and hope.

The letters to the Ephesians, Philippians, Colossians, and Philemon form a group and are associated with the period in which Paul was held captive in prison and yet still able to be in touch with his friends. His writing on freedom has a special poignancy in such a situation.

The two letters to the Thessalonians refer vividly to Christ's coming again. The sense of expectancy is strong and the picture of the imminence of a new age particularly vivid.

The three letters – two to Timothy and one to Titus – have quite a different tone and purpose. Called the 'Pastoral Epistles' they deal with the young church's organisation and discipline.

The letters bearing the names of John, Peter, James and Jude present us with a picture of the church in action, struggling, suffering, and facing not a little opposition. We see the church growing in confidence even at the cost of martyred lives.

The Epistle to the Hebrews, unlike the other New Testament letters, demonstrates in the form of a stylishly written and carefully presented treatise, the theme of Christ's priesthood. Here the continuity with the Old Testament is made clear, and the fulfilment of the promises is found in the vision of Christ as the great high-priest.

The four gospel narratives of Matthew, Mark, Luke and John tell in their distinctive ways the story of Christ's achievement. The approach of each is different. They do not claim to be biographies in the modern sense of biography: their concern is the personal identity of Jesus and his mission. Matthew deals with the conflict between Christianity and Judaism; Luke wrote for a wider public as his prefaces to his gospel and to his second volume, the Acts, indicate. The note of judgment sounds emphatically in Mark. John, as theologian, interprets the eternal significance of Christ's short ministry on earth.

The last book of the New Testament presents in the language of poetry and mystical vision the timelessness of the gospel. The beginning and the end are revealed in this Apocalypse of St John the Divine. The life of fellowship which exists between the church on earth and the church in heaven is movingly portrayed. The Revelation uncovers mysteries and unfolds the meaning of history, pointing to the significance of our life upon earth interpreted in terms of life eternal.

Dating the New Testament

The chronological order of the Books of the New Testament continues to be a matter under discussion. Scholars differ about the fixing of dates for the composition of the books.

The following list has met with considerable agreement, but it is clear that other views are constantly advanced with weighty arguments to lend them support.

Year	Epistles	Year	Gospels
A.D. 48/49	Galatians		
A.D. 50/51	1 and 2 Thessalonians		
A.D. 55-56	1 and 2 Corinthians		
A.D. 57	Romans		
A.D. 60-62	Ephesians		
	Philippians	A.D. 65-70	Mark
	Colossians		
	Philemon	A.D. 80	Luke - Acts
A.D. 64/65	1 and 2 Timothy		
	Titus		

A.D. 65-70	James	A.D. 80 Matthew
	1 Peter	
	1, 2, 3 John	
	Jude	
A.D. 90-100	Hebrews	A.D. 100 John
	Revelation	
125 A.D.	2 Peter	

When it is remembered that very few records of everyday events were kept in the days of Jesus of Nazareth, it is all the more remarkable that the principal manuscript evidence should date from a period as early as the fourth and fifth centuries A.D. Those who copied these manuscripts relied on earlier documents written not on vellum (skins) but on the more perishable papyrus. Excavators, unearthing fragments of papyrus texts during this century, have played an important part in the verifying of the text of the New Testament. A fragment of St John's gospel, dating from perhaps A.D. 130 is a striking example of early written evidence.

The gospel and the gospels

The word 'gospel' describes a new literary form among the biblical writings. In such early Christian writings as the Didache and the second epistle of Clement (c. A.D. 95), a gospel appears to be the name given to a written book. The word indicates 'good news', probably first passed on vocally and orally. Only later was the gospel committed to writing.

Before the good news was described in writing, it was spoken about in conversations, in answers to questions and in speeches. It had also a name 'kerygma' which meant a proclamation, delivered clearly and boldly very often in the manner of a herald 'reporting the news'. The essentials of the gospel or the proclamation included statements such as: 'Jesus is Lord; he is the Messiah, of David's line, he went about doing good, he was crucified, he was raised and is exalted, he will come in glory for judgment. Repent and be baptised; for forgiveness and the gift of the Spirit are available to you'.

The word 'gospel' originally meant 'a reward' or a 'gift'; that was good news. Then it meant the news itself. John makes no mention of it. Luke and Matthew do not use the word. The word 'gospel' appears many times in the other books of New Testament, often with such words prefixed to it as: the mystery of the gospel (Eph 6:19); the truth … (Gal 2:5,14); the hope … (Col 1:23); the faith … (Phil 4:15); or the word of the gospel (Acts 15:7). By the second century, however, in the time of Justin Martyr (c. A.D. 150) the 'evangel' or 'gospel' had come to mean a book about the life and teaching of Jesus.

The title probably came from Mark 1:1, 'the beginning of the gospel of Jesus Christ, Son of God'. This indicates that the starting point of the gospel is properly the work of John the Baptist. He is the last of the prophets, fulfilling Isaiah's premonitions, and the first of the new age prophets, a sort of Elijah come alive. The gospel here is more a message than a book. Because there was only one gospel, the usage 'the gospel according to Matthew, Luke, John', as well as Mark, was adopted.

When written, the four 'gospels', as records of the good news of Jesus Christ, according to Matthew, Mark, Luke and John, have the appearance of 'collections'. Sayings of Jesus, incidents in his life and ministry, as well as a more continuous narrative recounting his sufferings, trial and crucifixion, were eventually set down in writing and called 'gospels'.

We glean information about the written form of the gospel from such passages as the preface of Luke where 'many' writers are referred to; and also in John (21:25) where he mentions that all the books in the world could not contain what might be written on the subject.

CHAPTER 9

The Gospels and Acts

MATTHEW

Matthew has for long been a popular gospel. Placed first among the four evangelists, it has been thought, during the past 150 years, that Matthew drew upon Mark's material. It was not a case of Mark selecting extracts from Matthew.

Of the 28 chapters in Matthew, more than half contain virtually the same material as Mark (viz chapters 3, 8, 9, 12-17, 19-22, 24, 26-28). Some 200 verses of Matthew are like Luke. The special Matthew material stands out and accounts for the popularity of its themes and presentation.

This material includes:

(1) some of the beatitudes (chapter 5);
(2) the dramatic chapter 25 with its ' Inasmuch as you did it to the least of each of my brethren ye did it unto me';
(3) the fascinating journey of the Wise Men (chapters 1 & 2) and
(4) the farewell scene in Galilee after the resurrection (chapter 28): 'Lo, I am with you always'.

The masterly manner in which Matthew arranges and presents the message of the gospel has often been noticed. If the overall theme can be summarised as 'the coming of the kingdom of heaven' outlined for a Jewish audience, then the fulfilment of the Law, the emergence of the new Israel, and the urgency to heed the invitation to repent, are the main themes of this first gospel. The evangelist writes out of a community for a community.

The good news cannot escape without controversy. However good the healing and the teaching, the story of rejection and resistance is interwoven with this account of the judgements of Jesus and the uncompromising stand that he took in defence of his proclamation of the kingdom, which he affirmed had 'come upon' them. Those who recognise Jesus as Messiah will inherit the kingdom.

This evangelist was orderly in his editing. The writing of much that had been orally transmitted was clearly arranged for those under instruction.

Five collections of sayings can be discerned, providing a framework for a substantial body of teaching. 'When Jesus finished these sayings' (7:28), the crowd was astounded at the special authority with which he spoke, 'not like their scribes'.

While Jesus gave specialised instruction to his disciples (11:1), he went public with a message of popular challenge.

When he finished his parables (13:53), the teacher moved on and out from his home country on his further mission.

At chapter 19:1, Jesus finished another course of instruction, concerned with the nature of discipleship and the community life of believers.

In chapter 26, when on the threshold of the passion, Jesus concluded his programme of teaching confronting his listeners with parables of judgement (Ten Virgins, Talents, Sheep and Goats).

These five sections have been helpfully summarised by scholars on the following lines:

(1) 5-7   The sermon on the mount – heralding the kingdom
(2) 10   The sending of the twelve
(3) 13   Parables illustrating life in the kingdom
(4) 18   The nature of discipleship
(5) 23-25 The coming of the kingdom: what the kingdom of heaven will be like.

One of the features in his gospel shows Matthew may have been influenced by the atmosphere in Jewish circles at the time. This concerned the expectation that the 'end' would come soon. The apocalyptic language which refers to this has echoes from Daniel and the writings in the period between the Testaments as well as in the outlook of the Qumran community, as recorded in the Dead Sea Scrolls. 'When the Son of Man comes' (25:31) has a Daniel echo; so also have his references to 'angels' and 'the Son sitting on his throne in glory'. 'Before the Son of Man comes'

(10:23) has a similar urgency and foreboding. 'This generation' (24:34) would see it all. Some wonder if the destruction of Jerusalem in A.D. 70 coloured Matthew's presentation of this kind of prophetic announcement.

This gospel, with which the New Testament opens, is full of teaching. Yet the instruction given is particularly concerned with the answer to the question 'Who is Jesus?'

Matthew takes us back to the Old Testament in order to clarify the problems facing the people. He points out that Jesus was a man with a distinguished ancestry. The family tree of Joseph the husband of Mary (1:16) has familiar names, beginning from Abraham that 'father figure'; after 14 generations comes David 'king and anointed'; another 14 generations mark the period of monarchy ending with exile of the people in Babylon; 14 generations more and the Christ 'anointed and king' is born. Matthew summarises a long story; through this potted history, full of names set in a framework of numbered years, Matthew stresses that the nation's story is essential background reading for a proper understanding of the Christian gospel (chapter 1).

Jesus had among his titles both 'Christ' and 'Emmanuel'. It was the writer's conviction that God had been with his people through history in good times and in bad. Emmanuel meant 'God with us'(1:23). Jesus was a name that promised the saving of 'his people from their sins' (1:21). The Emmanuel of chapter one finds an echo in the final words of Jesus at the end of the gospel, 'Lo, I am with you always' (28:20).

The Old Testament reveals the promises which in the gospel find fulfilment. Matthew supplies quotations to illustrate the significance of Bethlehem as Christ's birthplace (2:6. Mic 5:2). The reference is messianic. The flight of the family into Egypt has special point: the reference is both Mosaic and prophetic (2:15, Hos 11:1). The slaughter of the innocents was also predictable (2:18, Jer 31:15). Even Nazareth, where Jesus was brought up, played a part in the fulfilment of prophecy from the past.

The teaching of Jesus is shown to have particular authority, when we consider his ancestry and his commission. Those titles, such as Son of God (4:3), Son of Man (12:8) and 'the Christ' (16:16), gave particular weight to his words.

Jesus taught his disciples. In his Sermon on the Mount, he did not intend to abolish 'the law and the prophets' (5:17). He did, however, introduce his teaching in a manner very different from the law-giving on another mountain long before. In addition to the commandments and statutes of Moses, Jesus 'opened his mouth and taught' in quite another style. He gave his listeners the Beatitudes (5:3-12). These were guidelines rather than laws. They encouraged attitudes of mind and heart. Those who were apparently not very happy or 'blessed' in the eyes of the world, became assured that blessedness deepened human experience and brought a new sense of wholeness to life. To be poor in spirit, to mourn, to be gentle, to forgive, to hunger and thirst for justice, to be 'pure of heart', to be a peacemaker, and even to suffer persecution, all these experiences and attitudes, which on the surface might seem to lack any joy, were in fact the key to a happily fulfilled life.

With the introduction, Jesus set the tone of his teaching (5:1-16). Then, using the old commandments as a basis, he proceeded to fulfil the law. There was more to the commandment 'You shall not kill' than could be expressed in the language of a legal code (5:21). Jesus had much more to say about angry attitudes, murderous thoughts, and hostile personal relationships. Sound and fair-minded as the old principle of 'an eye for an eye' may have appeared to be, Jesus startled his pupils with an unheard-of approach, the turning of the other cheek (5:39).

Some scholars have seen significance in the five collections of sayings, through which the evangelist sets out this new teaching of Jesus. Just as there were five books of Moses in the Law of the Old Testament, so in the following five sections Jesus appeared as 'a new Moses' (teaching sessions end at 7:28; 11:1; 13:53; 19:1; 26:1). Others do not attach particular importance to this arrangement of the gospel's teaching.

The teaching was soon followed by 'doing good'. Jesus healed (chapters 8 and 9). Both Jews and Gentiles were cured (8:10). Physical and spiritual illnesses alike were successfully treated; the crowds said 'never was anything like this seen in Israel' (9:33).

Choosing and training the twelve disciples followed (10:1). The teaching and healing were to continue in the new life which was compared with a kingdom. The prophetic words from Isaiah

were ringing true (Is 61; Mt 11:5). The description of the suffering servant (Is 42:1-4; Mt 12:18) fitted the teacher.

Jesus taught in parables rather than through formulae or defini-
tions. He illustrated life through pictures drawn from everyday
activities. The parable of the sower (13:18) has been called 'the
parable of the soils', in so many different ways is the seed received and allowed to grow. There is a timelessness about these
illustrations from the lives of farmers, fishermen, vine-dressers,
and merchants (chapters 13, 18, 22, 25).

On the way up to Jerusalem the passion narrative is introduced
with a strong note of judgement. Chapter 23 reveals the controversy stirred by the new teaching. If Jesus, through sermons,
healing acts, and human parables, points to life's blessings, he
also cries 'woe' to those who continue in greed and selfishness to
ignore the spirit of the Beatitudes and to make a mockery of the
kind of prayer which Jesus taught, addressing God as Father (6:9).

The sternness and indignation of chapter 23 stem from the
hypocrisy which he encountered. He told his disciples to 'practice and observe' whatever the scribes and the Pharisees, who sit
on Moses' seat, tell them, but not what they do (23:3), 'For they
preach and do not practise'. 'They do all their deeds to be seen
by men' (23:5).

Chapter 25, and in particular verses 31-46, are frequently quoted
in our day. They make crystal clear the importance of relating
prayer to action, expressing love through work as well as worship, perceiving that belief implies mutual responsibility in
God's world (25:35: 'I was a stranger and you welcomed me').

In the passion narrative, Matthew again draws on Old
Testament prophecy to bring out the significance of what is happening, 'the Son of Man goes as it is written of him' (Mt 26:24).
Matthew's story of the death of Jesus reveals something of the
tragic tensions involved in Christianity's separation from
Judaism. The crowd takes the blame for the death of Jesus onto
itself (27:25); the Jewish leaders plot to cover up the resurrection
(27:62-66; 28:11-15).

The news of the resurrection prompts responses across a wide
spectrum of emotion, reaching into the depths of human experi-

ence, 'with fear and great joy' (28:8). The final scene of the gospel climaxes in the great commission of the risen Jesus to his disciples: to bring the good news to all nations (28:18-20).

MARK

St Mark's gospel is the shortest of the four. Matthew has for many years been the favourite both for the general reader and the bible student. Mark has been attracting the scholar's attention recently for several reasons. Its importance has been increasingly recognised. It is also worth noting that ninety per cent of Mark's material is to be found in Matthew.

Mark is important on account of its probable early date. The writer's evidence of what happened in the life of Jesus has a reliable ring. It is not possible to be definite and accurate about the exact year in which this gospel reached its final form. Many agree that it was written shortly after the death of Peter, who with Paul suffered martyrdom in Rome. This took place in the emperor Nero's reign when the Christians became a target for persecution. Thus if Mark is placed in the years between A.D. 65 and 75, it is thought that it was written very probably in the earlier part of that ten-year period. For example, the manner in which the evangelist treats the destruction that befell Jerusalem in A.D. 70 (Mk:13), suggests that he was writing before the event. His narrative illustrates dramatically the insight of Jesus into what was happening politically and historically in his time.

Again, the close connection between the evangelist and St Peter lends a special authenticity to this gospel. Papias, an early bishop in Asia Minor mentions this link. In a fragment of writing dated about A.D. 140 we read: 'Mark, having become the interpreter of Peter, wrote down accurately all that he remembered of the things said and done by the Lord, but not however in order'. This quotation appears in the fourth-century history of the church written by Eusebius. Mark was probably written in Italy. There are signs that the evangelist had a good memory; even if his Greek is rough, the thinking behind the words appears to be eastern and Aramaic.

From a study of Mark, the meaning of the word 'gospel' is made clear. His opening sentence (1:1) suggests that a gospel was not in the first place a written document. 'The good news' would first have circulated from person to person. An oral tradition passed on the descriptions 'from mouth to mouth' of happenings, miracles, confrontations, and memorable sayings. Papias added: 'Mark made no mistake in thus recording some things just as he remembered them, for he made it his one care to omit nothing that he had heard and to make no false statement therein'. Mark put into writing what had been shaped by the community in various forms. The actual place in which the writing took place would also have considerable significance.

The message of this gospel was of prime importance. Mark does not claim to have produced a mere biography of Jesus. He does not, for example, record his birth and early childhood. He concentrates on what Jesus does and says.

Early as this gospel is in the history of Christianity, it is important to remember that the letters of St Paul were written before Mark. The Pauline emphasis on the death of Jesus and its meaning for the world may have influenced the gospel-writers, including Mark, as they treated 'the passion narratives' at length with considerable detail. Many think that the events of the passion were the first to be committed to writing.

Mark wrote in detail about the ministry of Jesus in Galilee. He writes anonymously. His gospel seems to have two parts:

(1) From chapter 1 - chapter 8:26. Here is a series of incidents, not necessarily in chronological order. They are presented straightforwardly with little comment. The events speak for themselves. Miracles, parables, teaching, and the coming of the Kingdom.

(2) Not until the second part is attention paid to the person of Jesus and his role as Messiah (chapter 8:31-end).

In between these two sections, the question put by Jesus to his disciples is asked, 'Who do men say that I am?' and the answer comes from Peter, 'You are the Christ' (8:27-30).

Then follows the move from Galilee to Jerusalem (10:1; 10:32). The transfiguration(9:2-8) and the foreshadowing of the cross point to the parables of judgement and prophecy spoken in Jerusalem (11, 12). In chapter 13, Jesus, in the only extended speech which Mark records, warns his hearers of wars, persecutions, doom, and 'the Son of man' coming with great power and glory (13:26). The language is 'apocalyptic', mysterious and yet revealing.

The passion and resurrection (14-16) are described with a stark simplicity. The sense of the loneliness is keenly felt. Jesus is depicted as a figure despised, rejected and abandoned (14:27: 'The shepherd is struck, the sheep scattered'; 14:50: 'All forsook him and fled'; 14:64: 'They all voted against him; 15:29: 'derided'; 15:31: 'mocked').

Mark, at the same time, conveys the message that God's purpose is over-riding. All that is happening at the trial and crucifixion is 'according to the scriptures' (Old Testament). (14:21: see Psalm 41:9; 14:27: see Zechariah 13:7; 14:49: 'Let the scriptures be fulfiled'; 15:34: see Psalm 22:1). The last supper (14:14) is prepared after Jesus asks, 'Where is my guest room, where I am to eat the passover with my disciples?' The inner meaning of that meal has clearly much to do with rescue, redemption, and covenant – the promises made by God to his people.

The ending of Mark with the words 'for they were afraid' (16:8) appears to be abrupt. There is a 'longer ending' (16:9-20). However, it is now very generally agreed that, since these extra verses are not found in the most reliable manuscripts (e.g. the codices *Sinaiticus* and *Vaticanus*, in particular), the placing of them in the margin and not in the text, as is done in the Revised Standard Version, is appropriate.

LUKE

Luke wrote with an eye on his readership. His was a two-volume work; the preface to the gospel matched by the introduction to Acts points to a common authorship.

The name of Luke was attached to the third gospel in the second century.

An able writer, he used the Greek language with a skillful flexibility. He caught the mood of the nativity and childhood of Jesus in his use of the biblical, poetical Greek of the Old Testament version, the Septuagint. While in the rest of the gospel he exhibits his literary talent, he shows also an ability to describe character and to express in forceful dramatic language the story he has to tell. His choice of words, and the colourful and imaginative style of his narrative, have often been noticed.

Coming possibly from Antioch, he wrote for the wide world. He saw that the events which took place in the life of Jesus of

Nazareth had meaning and relevance not alone for one country but for the whole human race. There was a universal message to be emphasised in the birth, suffering, trial, death and resurrection of the Christ.

In a time of misunderstanding and consequent opposition in many parts of the great Roman Empire, Luke sought to make clear that Christianity was not subversive nor yet anti-social in its life and practice. The Christians were not a threat to governments nor did they desire to be disturbers of the peace. On the contrary, they had a deep concern for the poor, the outcast, and for every single human being. They were more interested in people than in policies.

If Matthew laid emphasis on instruction in the faith with traditional methods, Luke aimed at the nations, the Gentile world, and his arrangement of his sources reflects this general objective. Matthew used 600 out of the 661 verses found in Mark, whereas Luke only used half of Mark's material. Matthew and Luke together use 200 verses not found in Mark, but drawn from a separate source. Again Luke and John have similarities which both share but which do not appear in Matthew or Mark.

Luke in his gospel prologue indicates his method of working. He informs us that many before him have compiled a narrative of the events. He, like them, received from eyewitnesses and official workers in the church what had been handed on. Luke was anxious to produce an orderly account for Theophilus, clearly, as his name suggests, an official in the imperial government, in order that he might know the facts and their credibility. We surmise a period of oral tradition, followed by a number of efforts made to record in writing the good news.

Luke, who can write in polished Greek and appears to have come from a Gentile background, nevertheless sees in the life and teaching of Jesus a clear fulfilment of the promises made in the Old Testament. So far from ignoring the Old Testament, he expresses the gospel in the idioms and language of Israel's past history. Jesus fulfils what Moses began; the death of Jesus is seen as a deliverance and redemption, and is called an 'exodus'. Many times in St Luke's gospel what has happened is recorded as 'what had to have happened'. Jesus had to be about his Father's business (2:49); he was sent to preach the good news

(4:43); he had to suffer many things and be rejected and killed (9:22; 17:25; 24:6-7). The scripture (i.e., of the Old Testament) had to be fulfilled in him (22:37). 'Everything written about me in the law of Moses and the prophets and the psalms must be fulfilled' Jesus said after his resurrection (24:44). Jesus's coming into the world is described as a 'visitation' (1:68). The place of the Holy Spirit also receives special mention in the Lucan narrative, indicating the destiny and the purpose of the life and ministry of Jesus (4:1).

Luke was once called 'the scribe of Christ's gentleness'. There was no reliable evidence that he used medical language in a technical way or indeed that he was, as tradition said, a physician, but clearly he brings out the compassion of Jesus for the sick and presents him as a healer. He writes with sympathy of the readiness of Jesus to forgive sinners that cause public scandal and have caused sinners to be outcast. The parables which are exclusively recorded in Luke and in his gospel narrative, but not in the other three, are often about people in trouble, who have deep spiritual needs, who have lost their way in life: e.g. the parables of the Good Samaritan (10:25), the Prodigal Son (15:11), the Pharisee and the Tax Collector (18:9), the Rich Fool (12:13), the Dishonest Steward (16:1), the Rich Man and Lazarus (16:19), the Widow and the Judge (18:1).

The evangelist sees a close connection between the Suffering Servant, described in Isaiah chapters 40-66, and Jesus facing crucifixion, proceeding on his journey up to Jerusalem. Jesus is given many titles in Luke, such as Son of Man, Saviour, Lord, Messiah, Son of God. The title Messiah or the Christ receives particular emphasis.

The phrase 'consolation of Israel' (2:25), the words of the *Nunc Dimittis* (2:29-32: a light to lighten the Gentiles), the voice crying, 'and all flesh shall see the salvation of God' (3:4-6), and Jesus's reading in the synagogue, 'The Spirit of the Lord is upon me' (4:18), and in the passion, 'he was reckoned among the transgressors' (22:37), all recall the role of the servant who suffered in order to bring comfort and healing, 'bearing the sin of many'.

The passion narrative in St Luke contains some features special to the writer. Luke shows us that there is an invisible spiritual conflict threading its course through the tragic events. Satan –

the power of darkness – enters Judas, and asks to have control of Simon Peter (22:3, 31, 53).

Through the darkness and gloom of all that is happening, Jesus manages to be in loving contact with those involved in the story. The right ear of the servant Malchus is healed (22:51). The Lord turns and looks on Peter after the denial (22:61). The weeping 'daughters of Jerusalem' are comforted when Jesus turns to speak to them (23:28).

From the cross, Jesus's words do not echo the phrases of Psalm 22 in the Lucan account. His compassion is rather intensified with 'Father, forgive ...' and those assuring words addressed to the penitent thief and the trustful 'Father, into thy hands ...'. The crowd, according to Luke, does not deride: it beholds. The centurion declares of the crucified that this was a righteous man. Out of the suffering, the love and healing shine.

JOHN

The Fourth Gospel is a gospel with a difference. The literary style, distinct and well-ordered, indicates a written rather than an oral tradition. The main events in the life of Jesus, their chronology, and their historical setting are all featured. Yet John gives us more than chronicle; his emphasis is upon the meaning of what took place. For example, the mighty acts of Jesus are not termed miracles but rather are seen to be signs. The lucid Greek of the author's writing and literary style express Jewish rather than Hellenistic thought. The whole narrative is set within the framework of the Jewish liturgical year; the Passover, the Feast of Tabernacles, and the feast of the Dedication all illustrate the significance of what Jesus says at those seasons and highlight the purpose of what happens to him.

This book may be divided into two parts with the headings: 'The Book of Signs' (2-12) and 'The Passion and Resurrection' (13-20) to describe them. The signs mark the relationship of the Old Testament with the revelation of the new. For example, new wine and old wine at the marriage in Cana of Galilee (2); bread of life instead of manna in the wilderness (6:31); the good shepherd (10:11); and the true vine (15) indicate the continuity between Israel and the new Israel.

The purpose of the author (20:31) is clearly stated. He wants his readers to believe that Jesus is the Christ, the Son of God, and that believing they may have life in his name.

He adds (21:25) at the end of his gospel that there are many other things that Jesus did. If they were written about, one by one, in the author's opinion the world could not hold the books that might be written about them.

If John's gospel appears to be written with a deeper sense of spirituality than is found in the other three gospels, it is well to remember that he is not by any means indifferent to the historical events which took place in the life of Jesus.

The phrase 'eternal life' is used to express the heart of the good news. Those who believe in Jesus will find 'eternal life'; it will be their salvation. It can be found and enjoyed already in this world; it is not confined to the future; it is a gift for the here and now (3:16, 36).

The birth of Jesus is described as 'the Word made flesh' (1:14). It is an event which forms the climax of the prologue in chapter 1. 'In the beginning was the Word' (1:1) introduces in the form of a hymn a profound meditation on the meaning of life, seen as relationship with God. This life is rooted in history.

The signs in the earlier part of the gospel demonstrate the connection between the temporal and the eternal. The wine of Cana is glory (2:11); the bread in the desert spells life (6:33); worship is more than local; the spirit and the truth of it are more important than the place where it is offered (4:24). Practical service to others is an essential part of the spiritual life (13:1-17).

In the discourses with his disciples (14-17), the special emphasis of this fourth gospel is made clear. What has been called the Johannine approach is the teaching given on the unity of Jesus with his heavenly Father (10:30). The union between Jesus and his disciples is also illustrated; the shepherd's relationship with his sheep (10) and the connection between the vine and the branches (15) indicate that 'being with Jesus', abiding in him (15:5), is of prime importance. In the prayer of Jesus with his disciples, this longing for the whole world to find a unity in truth and in holiness is expressed in such memorable intercessions as 'I do not pray for these only but also for those who are to believe in me through their word, that they may all be one' (17:20) and 'that they may become perfectly one, so that the world may know that thou hast sent me' (17:23).

In his passion narrative, John presents the trial and death as a story of victorious and creative suffering. Jesus is seen to be in control of all that was happening to him. There is a sense of divine purpose running through the gospel even before those critical days under Pontius Pilate (10:18: 'I lay down (my life) of my own accord'; 13:1: 'Jesus knew that his hour had come; 18:4: 'Jesus knowing all that was to befall him').

The glory of the cross shines through those dark days (17:1; 18:34-38; 19:17-30). Jesus judges Pilate. He carries his own cross (19:17). When he declares 'It is finished', it sounds like a cry of triumph (19:30). There is an awareness that Jesus is reigning from the tree.

After reading the end of this gospel, it is worthwhile returning to the prologue for a second reading of that first chapter. It summarises the whole gospel, historically and theologically. The words are short and concise; their meaning is inexhaustible; light, life, truth, grace are key words which interpret a gospel of love.

The question of the authorship of this fourth gospel is much discussed. Was the writer the disciple 'whom Jesus loved'? (13:23; 19:26; 20:2; 21:7, 20) He could have been John the son of Zebedee, a disciple standing by the cross (19:35). John was probably the last of the four gospels to be written. Scholars favour a date at the end of the first century, between A.D. 90 and 100.

ACTS

The Acts of the Apostles has sometimes been called 'the gospel of the Holy Spirit'. Not only in the second chapter is the power and the presence of the Spirit vividly illustrated, but in subsequent chapters it is the Spirit, rather than any individual Christian, which takes the initiative and becomes the driving force in the early church.

The language of Pentecost is universally understood. All sorts of nations from north, south, east and west, find a unity and a harmony. Each has a different language and culture but there is no confusion of tongues in the life of the Spirit. In fact, Babel was reversed at Pentecost. When the Spirit gave utterance to those who were in the house 'all together in one place' (2:1), the international crowd to their amazement found that 'each one heard them speaking in his own language' (2:6).

The life of the early Christians was lived in community. They did things together not because they were liable to be persecuted and inclined to be on the defensive. Far from withdrawing from the world, together they reached out to others with a freedom and a fearlessness that were quite remarkable. Not only were Peter and John 'bold' (4:13), but their kind of confidence was shared by all the faithful. This freedom of speech was not curbed but rather more fully emphasised when the Christians were thrown into prison and yet could not be muzzled.

The word 'faith' receives fresh prominence in Acts. Faith meant more than confidence or belief. It soon became the distinctive or technical expression for Christianity. If 'righteousness' was a key-word in the Old Testament, and 'knowledge' was the highest good among the Greeks, 'faith' summed up the Christian proclamation or kerygma. The content of the faith was the life, death, and resurrection of Jesus and also his exaltation. Perhaps the earliest creed or symbol of faith was the phrase 'Jesus is Lord'. Such a declaration was treasonable in an Empire where 'Caesar was Lord'.

The sense of mission is strong in Acts from the beginning. The numbers of those who were added to 'the common life in the Body of Christ' were recorded with some care. If the church began at Jerusalem, it continued in many centres: the list grows rapidly to include Samaria, Antioch, Cyprus, Asia Minor, Europe, Macedonia, Greece, Rome, and there is mention also of Spain. The Mediterranean world for many was the universe and the worldwide expansion of the faith which attracted both Jew and Greek, pagan and proselyte, became a fact. Its catholicity arose from application of the new life to all cultures and civilisations (Acts 17). The outreach of the church is described in terms of hazardous journeys, marked by interruptions and dangers of many kinds. The detailed description of the voyage of Paul to Rome included fierce winter storms and shipwreck. The safe arrival, against all expectation, in the face of the elements, pointed to the power of the Spirit to overcome such opposition.

The history of early Christianity expresses the theology of the new religion. The promises of the Old Testament are shown in the speech of Stephen to have found fulfilment in his day. His death, as first martyr, is marked with strange parallels to the death of Christ and becomes a starting point in the pilgrimage of Paul who stood by, consenting to the persecution, until the conscience-stricken moment of his conversion.

The missionary journeys, often traced on the map, are not lessons in geography. They describe spiritual experiences, not out of this world, but firmly rooted in the world of rivalries, jealousies, suspicion, fear and superstition. Acts provides 'life-situations' in which are revealed, in terms of persons and communities, both the challenges to the faith and the spiritual victories which reveal the glory of the faith.

Individual piety is not emphasised so much as community strength and the solidarity of the Christian fellowship. The continuity of the life in the Spirit, marked by steadfastness in prayer, meetings to break bread and to share eucharist, and the pooling of possessions prove to be of vital importance.

Peter and Paul are leaders. Acts is at pains to illustrate that, however different their temperaments and background, they are both 'one in the Lord' they serve, despite earlier controversy and a clash of personalities (Gal 2:11). Many other names are mentioned not so much for what they did but rather for what the Spirit accomplished through them; they were the right people in the right place.

In the organisation of the 'common life', function seemed to take precedence; a structured ministry came later. For example, the seven who were appointed to minister to the Hellenistic widows (6:1-6) were not actually called deacons, although their work was 'deaconing'. We read, too, of prophets and teachers at Antioch (13:1) as church life developed. Later at Ephesus (20:17) the elders, addressed by Paul, are also called 'overseers' (20:28); apparently the titles 'presbyter' (elder) and 'episcopos' (overseer, later translated as 'bishop') were at that stage interchangeable.

In the teaching, scriptural texts from the Old Testament were frequently quoted: while in Athens, Paul was quick to cite from the Greek classical philosophers and poets to make his point (Acts 17).

References to the servant, described in Isaiah, are applied to the 'servant Jesus' (3:13). The 'Anointed' of the Psalms underlines the message of the sermons preached in Jerusalem (4:26; Ps 2:2). With a special directness on the road to Gaza, Philip, when questioned about the suffering servant 'led as a sheep to the slaughter' (8:32), has an opportunity to help the Ethiopian courtier to understand what he is reading. Philip 'beginning with this scripture told him the good news of Jesus' (8:35).

Acts and Luke may have been one book with Luke as author. When, about the year A.D. 150, the Christians wished to have the four gospels in one book, Acts was probably separated. The so-called Muratorian canon indicates this: 'Moreover the Acts of all the Apostles are included in one book. Luke addressed them to the most excellent Theophilus, because the several events took place when he was present; and he makes this plain by the omission of the passion of Peter and of the journey of Paul when he left Rome for Spain.' This 'canon' has survived in an eighth-century translation of a second-century Greek original.

The date of Acts is thought to be after 64 A.D., the generally accepted date of Mark's gospel. Some suggest a later date between 70 and 80 A.D., although there is no mention of Paul's death. Luke uses 'we' in Acts 16:10-17; 20:5-15; 21:1-17; 27:1-28 when apparently quoting from his travel diary. He was thus an eye-witness of some of the events he reports.

The Book of Acts may be conveniently divided into six parts:

1.   1:1-6:7   Jerusalem – Peter
2.   6:8-9:31   Outreach to Palestine – Stephen, Philip, and the conversion of Paul
3.   9:32-12:24   Further outreach – Cornelius, the first gentile Christians
4.   12:25-16:5   Paul to Galatia and Jerusalem Council
5   16:6-19:20   Macedonia, Greece, Asia
6.   19:21-end   Voyage to Jerusalem, then to Rome – Paul a prisoner.

CHAPTER 10

St Paul's Letters

Traditional Order	Chronological Order	
	A.D.	
Romans	48/49	Galatians?
1 Corinthians	50/51	I Thessalonians
2 Corinthians		II Thessalonians
Galatians	55-56	Galatians?
Ephesians		I Corinthians
Philippians		II Corinthians
Colossians	57	Romans
1 Thessalonians	60-62	Philippians
2 Thessalonians		Colossians
1 Timothy		Philemon
2 Timothy		Ephesians
Titus	64/65	I Timothy
Philemon		II Timothy
		Titus?
		(*some date these three letters to about A.D. 100*)

Paul the Apostle

Saul of Tarsus in Asia Minor, later called Paul, was born c. A.D. 10. He was a citizen of the Roman Empire. He was brought up in his Jewish faith, 'a Hebrew of the Hebrews', of the tribe of Benjamin. He was educated in Jerusalem by Gamaliel, a Pharisee. His conversion on the road to Damascus was a turning point. On his way to persecute the Christians, he himself had a vision of Christ and became, as his letters show, a most ardent apostle of Christ and an outstanding expounder of the message and meaning of the Christian faith.

His letters to seven churches – Rome, Corinth, Galatia, Thessalonica, Philippi, Ephesus, and Colossae – reveal his personality. Further Pauline letters to Timothy, Titus, and Philemon contain valuable teaching and training as the life of the church develops through worship and ministry.

The dating and the authorship of the letters are frequent subjects of discussion. Two fixed dates in the history of the period are valuable guides in determining the chronology of the letters: Gallio, the proconsul at Corinth (Acts 18:12) held this office between May 51 and May 52 (as an inscription at Delphi testifies). Festus, who succeeded Felix as governor or procurator of Judea in the years 59 or 60, died two years later. Festus sent Paul to Rome in response to the apostle's appeal to Caesar. The date of Paul's death in Rome is probably A.D. 67. Thus, the letters that bear his name were all dispatched before the gospels were committed to writing.

THE PAULINE EPISTLES

Letters to seven churches

In the second letter of Peter, the last book of the New Testament to be written, there is a reference to the letters of the apostle Paul. 'Our beloved brother Paul' wrote according to the wisdom given to him about 'the coming of the day of God', the promise of 'new heavens and a new earth in which righteousness dwells'. The writer of 2 Peter adds this observation about all of Paul's letters: 'There are some things in them hard to understand, which the ignorant and unstable twist to their own destruction, as they do the other scriptures' (2 Pet 3:16).

From this it is apparent that the Pauline letters were already, quite early in the second century, considered as a collection of writings containing recognised and authoritative teaching. At the same time, what was written on a particular occasion to a local group of the faithful with problems in their own surroundings could easily be misinterpreted and adversely criticised.

It is important to reflect that these letters were not statements which contained systematic teaching, covering all the points of doctrine which might or might not be raised. They were often quite personal, written for the faithful; sometimes they were sent in answer to specific questions about conduct and belief. They are perhaps best understood as commentaries, presenting Christian thinking on a wide range of topics.

They are printed in the Bible not in chronological order, but according to their length. Romans, the longest of the letters, is placed first; the rest are in order of diminishing length.

ROMANS

The letter sent by Paul to the Romans is, in ways, more like a treatise than a personal communiqué. Written at a time when Nero was on the imperial throne, its probable date is A.D. 58.

In the capital city were Christians with both Jewish and Gentile backgrounds. Paul addressed himself to both cultures and is concerned to make clear the importance of the gospel for people of every culture.

Greek was the language widely used in Rome and also in the Mediterranean world. In eloquent Greek, Paul gives expression to the main theme of his letter when he writes: 'I am not ashamed of the gospel, because it is the power of God for the salvation of everyone who believes: first for the Jew, then for the Gentile for in the gospel a righteousness from God is revealed, a righteousness that is by faith from first to last' (Rom 1:16, 17).

This definition of the gospel he expounds in the first 8 chapters of his letter. Having declared the spiritual need which all human beings experience, whether Jews or pagans, he emphasises afresh (Rom 3:22): 'This righteousness from God comes through faith in Jesus Christ to all who believe'. He has linked the gospel with the teaching of the Old Testament and indicates that those who were brought up on 'the Law and the Prophets' had a great advantage (Rom 3:1). However, the good news is for all: 'There is no difference, for all have sinned and fall short of the glory of God and are justified freely by his grace through the redemption that came by Christ Jesus' (Rom 3:23, 24). Every word counts in a statement like this. Here is not only a definition of sin, 'a falling short of God's glory', but also the meaning of the Bible is summed up as 'the story of the redemption of human life' by God.

The word 'justifies' is further elucidated in the eighth chapter of this letter. If justification appears to have strong legal overtones, it is clearly concerned with the status which the human being has in the presence of God who is a God both of justice and of love.

Paul outlines in memorable language the standing of the 'creature' in the presence of a faithful creator: 'We know that in all
things God works for the good of those who love him, who have
been called according to his purpose. For those God foreknew
he also predestined to be conformed to the likeness of his Son,
that he might be the firstborn among many brothers. And those
he predestined, he also called; those he called, he also justified;
those he justified, he also glorified' (Rom 8:28-30). God's initiative is constantly emphasised; his grace perfects nature.

Chapter 8 marks the climax of this exposition of the Christian
gospel. There are technical words which express both belief and
experience. Paul, with his background as 'a Hebrew of the
Hebrews', sees in the words he uses a new significance as a result
of the crucifixion and resurrection of Jesus.

In chapters 9-11, Paul pays special attention to the history of
Israel, the message of Moses (Rom 10:5) and the calling of the
remnant (Rom 11). The goodness and the severity of God are
mingled together in the story of salvation (Rom 11:22).

The remainder of the letter (Rom 12-16) points out the implica-
tions of this goodness of God's righteousness. The 'therefore' at
the beginning of chapter 12 declares that the theological thinking outlined in the earlier chapters prompts the faithful to put
this kind of life into practice. Personal dedication (12), good citi-
zenship and a right relationship with the state (13), combined
with concern for the welfare of the weak and needy, must follow
upon the acceptance of the gospel.

Towards the conclusion of the letter, Paul, who has not yet visited
Rome, states his great desire to make the journey and to be with
those to whom he has written the letter (Rom 15:32). Even if
some scholars consider chapter 16 to be a separate addendum,
this chapter's personal message, with a long list of individual
names, illustrates that the love of God, so eloquently described
in chapter 8 and elsewhere, must ultimately find expression in
human relationships and the personal affection that characterises
these parting words of greeting.

I CORINTHIANS

Paul had spent eighteen months in Corinth in the early fifties. His letter, 1 Corinthians, was apparently written from Ephesus sometime between A.D. 55 and 57. It deals with certain quest- ions raised by the Christian community. Paul in his reply gives directions about many points, some concerning Jewish cere- monies, others dealing with the unity of the church and more than a few moral problems facing Christians in a sea-port town, with its cosmopolitan population.

The questions raised and, in this letter, considered and answered, included points about church authority and the risk of schisms within the worshipping community. Parties had sprung up even at that early stage (1:10; 3:4, 5). This controversial subject, how- ever, gave Paul the opportunity of teaching about Christ cruci- fied, 'the wisdom and power of God' (1:24), and also about the Holy Spirit (2:10–16). In addition, many moral problems receive Christian answers: these include cases of incest, fornication, and marriage difficulties (5, 6, 7). Anxieties about eating food sacri- ficed to idols reflect the kind of mixed society of pagans and be- lievers in which the faithful lived. Important instruction of a positive kind is then given by Paul in some outstanding chapters of permanent worth for Christians of every age. These include teaching on the eucharist (11), on life in the Spirit as church members with varied gifts (12), the famous hymn of a love, greater even than faith and hope (13) and the all-important ex- position of the resurrection (15).

This letter, rich in doctrine, with many phrases made familiar by frequent quotation, serves as a guide to the solving of current problems of personal relationships, unhappy Christian rivalries and divisions, and some understandings concerning both the Old Testament (10) and the workings of the Holy Spirit (14).

II CORINTHIANS

This has been called 'an epistle of conflict'. Often, out of suffer- ing and controversy, faith is strangely strengthened and the un- pleasant experience (whatever it might be) creates new under- standing. Sorrow is turned into joy. This is certainly one of the lessons of the second letter.

It is a letter which has a puzzling structure. Many think that there is more than one letter in the text of these 13 chapters.

There are commentators who trace no fewer than four separate communications:

(1) 2:14-7:4 might be called 'a letter of defence'

(2) 1:1-2:13, and 7:5-6 'a letter of reconciliation'

(3) 8-9 'a letter of recommendation'

(4) 10-13 'a severe letter'.

(1) The 'letter of defence' seems to hint that the ministry of Paul has been criticised and his authority questioned. This produced some profound teaching about ministry. Paul is a minister of the New Testament or covenant (3:6), not of the letter, but of the Spirit. He calls his correspondents his letter (3:2: 'you yourselves are our letter'). The result of his ministry is written 'not on tablets of stone but on tablets of human hearts' (3:3). Christians do not preach themselves, 'but Jesus Christ as Lord, and ourselves as your servants' (4:5). We also have the treasure of the gospel 'in earthen vessels' (4:7). There is a striking note of humility in the writer's description of his work. Ministry is not human achievement but God's gift: 'God gave us the ministry of reconciliation' (5:18).

(2) The' letter of reconciliation'. It is difficult to know the particulars of the breakdown in relationships between the apostles and the Christians of Corinth. Paul's attitude is firm and yet conciliatory. 'I call God as my witness,' he wrote, 'that it was in order to spare your feelings that I did not return to Corinth. We are not dictators over your faith, but are fellow workers with you for your happiness ... I made up my mind not to pay you another painful visit' (2:1). Later Paul added: 'I see that my letter hurt you ... I am happy now, not because I made you suffer, but because your suffering led to your repentance' (7:8).

(3) In chapters 8 and 9, Paul tells the Corinthians that he is sending Titus and some others to them, and recommends them to the Corinthians as worthy of welcome and respect. The purpose of this visit by Titus is to receive a contribution from the Corinthian Christians for their poor brethren in Jerusalem. These chapters are a reminder that solidarity with one another, and especially care for those less fortunate than ourselves, are intrinsic to the Christian faith. The collection among Paul's gentile converts for the welfare of poor Jewish believers in

Jerusalem was an important demonstration of the new unity of Jew and gentile in faith in Christ. Paul appeals to the Corinthians to give generously. He reminds them of the supreme example of Christ's grace, 'that though he was rich, yet for your sake he became poor, so that by his poverty you might become rich' (8:9).

(4) The 'severe letter' contains such phrases as 'let no one take me for a fool' (11:16); 'Let me do a little boasting of my own'. The tone of these final chapters is quite changed. There follows the famous description of his sufferings: 'Thrice was I beaten with rods, once was I stoned, three times I was shipwrecked ...' (11:25). In spite of the boasting style, he is essentially dependent on God who said to him, 'My grace is sufficient for you, my power is made perfect in weakness' (12:9). Suffering and weakness are memorably interpreted by the lessons of the cross of Christ: 'He was crucified through weakness, and still he lives now through the power of God' (13:4).

The whole epistle, whether fragmentary or not, is suitably summed up in the words of 'the Grace' familiar in liturgy and worship (13:14).

GALATIANS

Paul writes to the faithful in Galatia on hearing that they have been persuaded that it is necessary for a Christian to keep all that is commanded in Jewish law. He sums up his argument with the words (2:16): 'We have believed in Christ Jesus, in order to be justified by faith in Christ, and not by works of the law, because by works of the law shall no one be justified.'

The letter is written somewhat defensively. Paul finds he must explain what happened in his own life: details are given of his conversion, his time of retreat in Arabia, and then of his acceptance by the apostles in Jerusalem (1:15-24).

At one point, his authority needs to be asserted. Paul writes that he opposed Peter 'to his face' (2:11) on the subject of 'circumcision'. Paul, in reply to the views of the 'circumcision party' (2:12), which required the observance of this Jewish rite, said to Peter, 'If you, though a Jew, live like a Gentile and not like a Jew, how can you compel the Gentiles to live like Jews?' (2:14).

Valuable teaching on authority supplies answers to important questions about the faith. For example, the gospel is not man-made (1:11); there is only one gospel (1:7); it is given to every one, including Paul himself, through Jesus Christ.

In chapter 3, Paul writes about Abraham's faith in days long be-fore the Law (3:17). He sees here hard evidence that no one is justified before God by the law, for 'he who through faith is righteous shall live' (3:11, quoting Habakkuk 2:4).

'To be justified' means 'to be acquitted', 'to be declared innocent or right'. Justification (or righteousness) is an Old Testament word which denotes the standing or status a person has when appearing before a judge in court. This word also expresses a quality of relationship, depicting right standing in relation to God.

When the question was asked 'why have a law?' (3:19), Paul replied: 'Before faith came we were imprisoned by law, until faith should be revealed. So that law was our custodian until Christ came.'

Later in the letter to the Romans this teaching about justification is further developed. Both Galatians and Romans indicate that no one is justified by his own works (Rom 3:28, Gal 5:4, 5).

This important message to the Galatians concerns their life in the Spirit. 'Walk in the Spirit,' he writes, 'and to not desire to gratify the desires of the flesh' (5:16). 'If you are led by the Spirit you are not under the law' (5:18). There is a new freedom but it must be used with love and not selfishness (5:13). There is a sense in which the whole law is fulfilled in one phrase, 'You shall love your neighbour as yourself' (5:14). 'Bear one another's burdens and so fulfil the law of Christ' (6:2).

A high-light of the letter is the classical list of the fruits of the Spirit: love, joy, peace, patience, kindness, goodness, faithful-ness, gentleness, self-control. Paul adds, 'Against such there is no law' (5:22, 23).

The Galatians were neighbours of the Phrygians and Cappa-docians. They were descended from celtic tribes who migrated from central Europe to settle in Asia Minor about the third cen-tury B.C. Galatia was made a Roman province in 25 B.C. It is not certain if the Galatians whom St Paul addressed in his letter included those living in the larger area extending southwards to include Iconium, Lystra and Derbe, places visited by him on his second missionary journey. Galatia may perhaps have been used in this wider sense. No firm conclusion has been reached in this question of the identity of these Galatians. The letter was probably written around A.D. 56, although some scholars think it is one of Paul's earliest letters, written around A.D. 49.

EPHESIANS

This Pauline picture of the church is impressively painted in memorable phrases and flowing style. The description sums up in positive terms the unity of the church, its power to promote love and peace, its expression of the reconciling life of Christ in the world.

Apparently written from prison, the letter contains references to the writer's captivity (4:1; 6:20). In spite of this, the joy and hope of the gospel are uppermost in the description of the church as the Body of Christ. There is mention of the cross but a marked emphasis on the exaltation of Christ. The instructions given to the members of the 'body' indicate that a living and expanding future lies ahead for the church. Marriage and the obligations of husband and wife in partnership are seen to symbolise the union between Christ and his church (5:21-33). The care and education of children are essential for the continuity of the faith (6:1-4).

There is little mention of any controversy in this letter which reads more like a considered and carefully expressed statement of church teaching rather than a personal communication. The RSV places the reference to Ephesus in the margin rather than in the text of the epistle (1:1); some important manuscripts make no mention of Ephesus; this has led scholars for many years past to suggest that the letter was designed to be circulated among a number of churches. A general statement about the unity, the origins, and the nature of the church are set out; particular problems are not to the fore. It is true that a reference is made to the tension that often existed between Jew and Gentile, but the breaking down of the barrier, 'the middle wall of partition', is the good news. There are also dark references to prevalent 'impurity and covetousness'; these are succeeded by encouraging words about 'the light of Christ' and the vision of a church 'without spot or wrinkle or any such thing'.

The epistle is frequently quoted when the unity of the church is under discussion: chapter 4 still inspires those who endeavour to maintain 'the unity of the Spirit in the bond of peace' (4:3). The holiness of the church and its power to renew the lives of those who 'learn Christ' (4:20) demonstrate how evil can be overcome by goodness and love. The church is like a building. Jews and other nationalities are no longer strangers or temporary occupants of 'the household of God'. The foundations are the apostles and the prophets, 'Christ Jesus himself being the chief corner-stone' (3:20). These 'notes' of the church, listed later in formal creeds, can be found in this buoyant account of the unity, holiness, apostolicity, and catholicity of 'the Body of Christ'.

Ephesus was a significant recipient of such a universal message. Paul had spent three years there, championing the faith and tasting bitter opposition. From this capital of the proconsular province of Asia, one of the largest cities of the Roman world, this impressive statement of the Christian way may well have been issued to many other centres.

PHILIPPIANS

Paul writes in a more personal vein to the members of the first European church which he founded. Philippi is described in Acts 16:12 as 'the leading city of Macedonia, and a Roman colony'. Whereas Ephesians had been impersonal, with scarcely any names mentioned, Philippians is warm-hearted (1:7) with greetings extended to friends and individuals (4:1, 2, 3).

This is one of the letters from prison, sent probably from his captivity in Rome. Some have suggested that it might have been written from his time in prison at either Ephesus or Caesarea.

Personal suffering can be detected between the lines of this 'martyr' epistle (4:11). For Paul, to live is Christ and 'to die is gain' (1:21). Humility and hope triumph: in spite of his plight, he presses on 'toward the goal for the prize of the upward call of God in Christ Jesus' (3:14).

He urges his readers to think positively about what is honourable, just, pure, and lovely (4:8). He warns them about the opposition; the old dispute about circumcision still lingers (3:2). It is important to be united in the church's work (4:2).

A statement about the incarnation of Christ, made to illustrate his humility in chapter 2, has become important in the subsequent history of Christian creeds and liturgy. This passage in the text draws attention to the pre-existence of Christ before his birth in Palestine: 'He was in the form of God' (2:6); 'He emptied himself, taking the form of a servant, being born in the likeness of men' (2:7). This was a unique and outstanding example of humility. Furthermore, after the humiliation of death by crucifixion, God highly exalted Jesus (2:9). These points clearly made about the incarnation were to be quoted in later controversies when many varied and, in the eyes of the church, heretical opinions about the humanity and divinity of Jesus Christ were debated. The whole statement (2:5-11) has been used in Christian worship as a hymn or a creed. There is a liturgical ring about its phrasing. These verses were easily memorised and set to music. Similarly in 4:4-7, Paul's words of praise were often to be repeated in worship.

COLOSSIANS

The church at Colossae in Asia Minor, not far from Ephesus, was founded by Epaphras, not by Paul (1:7). The letter to the Colossians contains much of the teaching of Ephesians. The main subject of Ephesians was the church. The thrust of Colossians is towards a deeper understanding of the person of Christ.

Colossians, also a prison-letter, expounds the relationship of Christ to God, to the creation, and to the church. 'He is the image of the invisible God, the first-born of all creation' (1:15). 'All things were created through him and for him' (1:16). 'He is the head of the body, the church' (1:18).

Such statements are made with a particular explicitness, because certain doctrines were circulating in Colossae at the time which needed to be countered. Among them were angel-worship (2:18), rules about diet and the observance of new moon festivals and sabbaths (2:16), as well as extremes of asceticism (2:23). Some of these practices had the appearance of wisdom but they were not 'according to Christ'. They were but shadows of what is to come; the substance belongs to Christ (2:17).

The reference to 'philosophy' (2:8), which in Paul's view was misleading the people, may have arisen from the prevalence of the so-called 'gnostic' approach to spirituality. The word 'gno-sis' ('knowledge') was used to describe a system of thought which called 'matter' evil and separated it entirely from 'spirit'. Such a separation or 'dualism' would undermine the teaching about Christ's redemption and the belief that 'the Word was made flesh'. Hence Paul's insistence that in Christ 'the whole fullness of deity dwells bodily' (2:9). Sin was more than ignor-ance, bewilderment or lack of 'knowledge'; sin separated the sinner from God on account of disobedience and pride.

It has become apparent, since the discovery of the Qumran scrolls, that the errors hinted at in chapter 2 arose from a con-fused mixture of pagan, Jewish and Christian ideas about cre-ation and the problems of evil.

The letter closes with a request for its contents to be read in the nearby cities of Laodicea and Hierapolis. It was important for more than one place in Asia Minor to learn about the new life in Christ, that 'here there cannot be Greek and Jew, circumcised and uncircumcised, barbarian, Scythian, slave, free man, but Christ is all in all' (3:11).

I AND II THESSALONIANS

The first letter to the faithful in Thessalonica, the capital city of Macedonia, introduces Paul's way of greeting and teaching at one and the same time.

His own experiences in that city, described in Acts 17:1-10, were turbulent. The Jewish population had stirred a riot and driven him out. 'We were torn away from you' (2:17), Paul writes to the Christians whom he praises for their steadfastness in times of af-fliction and persecution (1:6). He emphasises the point that the gospel is not merely a matter of words: it comes alive in people and their conduct (1:8). The letter is written in the warmest and most affectionate of terms: Paul surprisingly compares himself with a mother caring for her little children (2:7).

There are, however, two important pieces of teaching in the let-ter. First, he warns against the local idolatry: licentiousness and sexual immorality are closely associated with this false worship (4:3-8). Secondly, he speaks encouragingly of the coming of the Lord, and seems to indicate that it would be sooner rather than later (4:17).

The second letter has more information about the Lord's coming. It was written very shortly after the first. Both are usually dated about the year A.D. 50. Paul is anxious that his words about 'the Lord's coming' will not be taken out of context. He has heard that the Christians have given up their work as a result and have fallen into sheer idleness, waiting as it were for the dramatic end (2 Thess 3:6ff). Paul explains that much has to happen before 'the day' arrives. He mentions cryptically 'the lawless one' and 'the rebellion' (2:3). There is much discussion and uncertainty about this kind of mysterious, apocalyptic language. Suggestions have been made associating 'the lawless man' with tyrants of contemporary history. The 'rebellion' or 'apostasy' (2 Thess 2:3) was prophesied when the subject of 'the end of the world' was discussed (see Mt 24 where there is mention of 'wars and rumours of wars' which must happen 'but the end is still to come').

It is interesting to note that the actual phrase 'the second coming' is not used in the New Testament. This was coined later. There is a reference in the epistle to the Hebrews (Heb 9:28) to the time when Christ 'will appear a second time'. The 'coming', however, is very much part of the faith in its wholeness. The word means 'the presence' (*parousia*, in Greek). Paul is emphatic that it should not be dreaded, but rather is something to be welcomed in the future. He wrote of 'the splendour of the parousia' (2 Thess 2:9) but urged the Thessalonians not to become too excited about it (2 Thess 2:2) as though the day had already come. The word has royal overtones and was used of the arrival of a monarch. The sense of Christ's presence, experienced at the transfiguration, was still with the Christians in the early years of the church (2 Pet 1:16).

THE PASTORAL EPISTLES

The letters to Timothy and Titus are called 'pastoral' since they contain practical instructions to these church leaders about the teaching, worship, and personal service in the life of the church.

Timothy in Ephesus and Titus in Crete have the task of organising the corporate and community life of the Christians.

The events referred to are not covered by the narrative of the Acts of the Apostles. A later date is often assigned to these personal letters; in the opinion of some they were written about the year A.D. 100. Scholars differ over the question of authorship. Some believe that they were written or compiled by a former student of Paul's who showed himself thoroughly familiar with Paul's teachings. If they are not entirely by Paul in the form in which they appear, they are Pauline, and many who have studied the style and the unusual vocabulary, suggested that at any rate there are many Pauline fragments, paragraphs and quotations in these manuals of instruction. For example, the use of the word 'saying' (1 Tim 1:15; 4:9; 2 Tim 2:11) prompts the thought that statements very like creeds in the germ were known by heart and were used both in the course of teaching and also in worship.

There are fragments of hymns also in the text (1 Tim 3:16; 2 Tim 2:11-13) which throw light in an interesting way upon the development of a liturgy at an early stage. Worship is analysed and arranged under such headings as requests, wishes, intercessions, and thanksgivings (1 Tim 2:1). Ministry is also ordered and the portraits of the bishop and the deacon (1 Tim 3) illustrate the standards of character and behaviour expected. Furthermore, personal service given to widows, elders, and slaves (1 Tim 5 and 6) is seen as an important pastoral responsibility. Not only is sound doctrine an urgent matter requiring attention in the midst of some prevailing myths and superstitions (1 Tim 6:3f), but charitable caring of persons in need of help is also a pressing Christian duty (1 Tim 5:10).

There are fewer references to the central beliefs of the Christian Church in these letters. There is scarcely any mention, for example, of the cross and its significance, apart from an impressive phrase: 'There is one God and one mediator between God and men, the man Christ Jesus, who gave himself as a ransom for all' (1 Tim 2:5). This serves as a headline for the summoning of everyone to true worship, soundly ordered.

The place of the study and use of the scriptures in the life of the church during these early formative years illustrates the conviction that the Old Testament promises were fulfilled in Christ: Timothy is told to continue in what he had learned from infancy in 'the holy scriptures which are able to make you wise for salvation through faith in Christ Jesus' (2 Tim 3:15).

PHILEMON

This short, personal letter written by Paul from prison throws light in an interesting and intimate way upon early Christian life at the local level.

Philemon, to whom the letter was addressed, seems to have been one of Paul's converts, living at Colossae (in verse 19, Paul wrote 'you owe me your very self'). Philemon's slave, Onesimus, apparently ran away from his master and had possibly been suspected of stealing (verse 18). Paul came to know this slave, who under his influence became a changed character. Onesimus means 'profitable' and Paul writes that he really has proved 'profitable', living up to his name and is now more like a son than a slave. The letter urges Philemon to receive the runaway and have him back for good (verse 15) as a dear brother.

Although slavery could not be abolished or even reformed by Christian action in that period of the Roman empire, humane and loving treatment of servants in a household of faith or a 'house church' (verse 2) could make them welcome members in quite a new way (verse 17). The decision about accepting Onesimus must be Philemon's. Paul, with his own hand (verse 19), writes most persuasively but does not attempt to force the issue (verse 14). In personal relationships the Christian gospel had power to transform family and domestic life.

CHAPTER 11

The Other Letters and Revelation

THE EPISTLE TO THE HEBREWS

This is not so much a letter as an instruction. There are few personal greetings. As a discourse about the priesthood and sacrifice of Jesus, it is addressed to second-generation Christians who are in danger of falling away from the faith. Some are longing to return to the ceremonial ways of worship associated with their Jewish background. Others with a Greek view of life are attracted by the philosophical approach to things eternal. This epistle has been called a 'bridging' letter. Both Hebrew expression of the faith 'from times past, through the prophets' (1:1) and Greek phrasing for faith 'as the substance of things hoped for, the evidence of things not seen' (11:1) combine to deliver the message of the gospel to the Mediterranean world.

Hebrews interprets the historical account of the life and death of Jesus. His presence in the world continues. 'We see Jesus' (2:9). 'Jesus Christ is the same yesterday, and today, and for ever' (13:8).

Jesus is called a priest. This is the word used to show that he completes and fulfils the laws and prophecies of the Old Testament. He is not compared with Aaron in the days of Moses, but more mysteriously, the uniqueness of Jesus is illustrated by the more shadowy figure of Melchizedek (5:10), who was 'after an eternal order' with origins that remain obscure. The priesthood of Jesus is inevitably connected with his sacrifice.

The concept of priesthood is not narrow, but rather it is representative. The risen and ascended Christ offers to the Father the life which has passed through death (9:24). His sacrifice does not only mean his death but also the offering of his life (9:20). It was once for all. Christians look back to the death of Jesus but they also look up to him 'who ever lives to make intercession' for them (7:25). Intercession is more than prayer offered for others; it is a giving of self or, as it has been described, 'a moral movement'. If priesthood is the character of the Son of God, through whom God made the world (1:2), then all creation is intended to have this character of being concerned with all life, of reaching out in love and faith to all.

The message of the letter urged 'the Hebrews' to have a better possession, the realities which abide. This can be done by faith, by work, and by sacrifice.

(1) Faith is not only defined (11:1) but is seen in action through the lives of former faithful figures, beginning with Abel, including Noah, and especially Abraham. Many others were faithful including to our surprise Rahab (11:31) and predictably the Judges and prophets (11:32). Many without names bore their witness, suffering men and women 'of whom the world was not worthy' (11:38).

(2) Work included good deeds (10:24), but also public worship and community action (10:25). It also involved peace-making (12:14) and upholding standards of behaviour (12:15).

(3) Sharing in the sacrifice of Jesus is pictured movingly and poetically in chapter 12:22-24.

The date of the letter may have been in the time of the emperor Domitian's persecution (A.D. 95). It is quoted by Clement of Rome (c. A.D. 95), who gives no hint of its authorship.

JAMES

This 'general' statement about Christian life and behaviour is addressed to Jewish Christians dispersed through the Mediterranean countries (1:1), perhaps in particular Egypt and Syria.

There are only two direct references to Jesus (1:1; 2:1) yet the teaching and counselling contain many echoes of the Sermon on the Mount (Mt 5-7). There is also a distinct flavour of the 'wisdom' found in such books as Ecclesiasticus and Proverbs. The readers of this homily are urged to be swift to hear, slow to speak, slow to be angry (compare 1:19 with Ecclus 5:11). James is a practical guidebook of moral advice and exhortation, but the style is far from dreary. Vivid illustrations drive home the importance of sincerity and an awareness of the needs of others.

The poor are praised; the rich are warned (2:5f). 'Love your neighbour' is a royal law found in scripture (Lev 19:18 quoted in Jas 2:8).

The examples which the writer urges his readers to follow are taken from the Old Testament. Abraham's faith was demonstrated by his wholehearted obedience (2:21-23). Job's patience and perseverance in the midst of trials and temptations were exemplary (5:11). Elijah, a very ordinary person with little of this world's goods or power, is a strong reminder of the effectiveness of prayer (5.17).

It may seem strange that there is no mention of the crucifixion of Jesus nor of his resurrection. This document may have been composed in the early sixties of the first century A.D. Statements about the meaning of the faith did not find expression in the form of an official creed in James. The famous declaration that faith is dead unless it is followed up by action has been much discussed. James and Paul had different approaches when expounding the nature of faith. They were not necessarily contradicting each other. Paul explained 'faith' as a gift from God, setting the believer in a right relationship with God. James contrasts a 'belief' that is in the mind or on the lips with the dynamic of 'personal trust'. Perhaps both James and Paul could have agreed on this familiar summary of the argument: 'Faith alone justifies, but not faith which is alone'.

Sincerity is urged by James throughout the five chapters. Trials and testings help the growth of faith and are to be welcomed (1:2). There is all the difference between worldly and heavenly wisdom (3:13). Small things wisely handled can be surprisingly powerful. For example, the rudder of a ship, the spark that starts a fire, and the bit in the horse's mouth. With such colourful examples from everyday life, James urges his readers to control their tongues (3:2-12), to be open and honest with each other (5:16) and to discover the power of prayer. His definition of true religion (1:27) is both social and personal (while keeping self unspotted, the duty of caring for widows and orphans must not be neglected).

I PETER

Peter, helped by Silas, writes a circular letter to Christians in a number of centres in Asia Minor (5:12; 1:1). Mention is also made of Mark. They are evidently in Rome. The city is called Babylon at the close of the letter (5:13, as is the case in Revelation 17).

Those to whom this first letter of Peter is addressed are living in pagan surroundings and are evidently in great need of encouragement. They are suffering on account of their faith and they have to face and resist many trials and temptations. The letter expounds the faith in positive and warm-hearted terms (1:3f). It is full of hope and praise in view of what God has done for the people of the world through the suffering and resurrection of Jesus Christ.

It is important, therefore, for Christians to realise who they are. The memorable description of their calling and their role is encapsulated in four short phrases: they are 'a chosen race, a royal priesthood, a holy nation, a special people' (2:9). With these privileges, there are accompanying responsibilities. Therefore the letter includes instruction about conduct and attitudes: good behaviour in pagan surroundings will silence the opposition (2:12, 15).

The sufferings of Christ, when considered, are shown to have had meaning and purpose. Those who receive the letter are urged to rejoice that they are called upon to share in Christ's sufferings (4:13). This difficult subject of suffering is handled by the writers of the letter with a special sensitiveness (3:8-22). If people have a clear conscience, if they are ready to stake all their hopes on the future, if they behave with gentleness and respect for others, they may have to suffer. Christ's suffering brought people to God and showed in a unique way what the righteous could do for the unrighteous (3:18).

This letter contains a difficult and somewhat mysterious section about Christ 'preaching to the spirits which were in prison' (3:18). This has been interpreted as the opportunity given to those who lived and died before Christ's death of sharing in the forgiveness and reconciliation of the cross. Even those who perished in the flood of Noah's time were not forgotten (3:19). There is vivid symbolism mingled with an interpretation of the mean-

ing of baptism in this part of the letter. Christ, in the interval between his death and resurrection, showed that his sacrifice for
the unrighteous was all-inclusive.

Surprise has been expressed that a letter from Peter had no personal references to the days in Galilee which he spent with
Jesus. The style of the letter is literary; sound doctrine is often
expressed in liturgical language. Old Testament sources are
used to illustrate the new life of holiness, and the church, built
of people wherever they might be, consisting of individuals as
'living stones' (2:5). This has led to the view that the letter had a
combined authorship, written perhaps about the year A.D. 64,
at a critical time of approaching martyrdoms, when the sense of
'the end' was keenly felt (4:7).

II PETER

Of all the New Testament documents the 'Second Epistle of
Peter' is the latest. Addressed to Gentile Christians in Asia
Minor, its probable date is c. A.D. 140. It was not included in the
'Muratorian' list of New Testament books.

The reference to the transfiguration 'on the holy mount' links
the name of Peter with this letter (1:18). That spiritual experience is quoted as firm evidence of 'the power and coming of the
Lord', illuminating subsequent thinking about the parousia.

The style of the letter seems to be influenced much more by
Jude than 1 Peter. False teachers are challenged dramatically.
Scoffers had derided the idea of 'a second coming', and had
asked with sharp sarcasm 'when will it be?' 'Where is the
promise of his coming?' (3:4). The answer is confident that it
will come as 'a thief in the night' (3:10), but it is important,
when considering the timing, to remember that 'one day is with
the Lord as a thousand years' (3:8).

The false teachers claimed to have special knowledge. This
'knowledge' in the Hellenistic world was very different from
'the knowledge' that came from Christ (1:3). Christians are described in the impressive phrase as 'partakers of the divine nature', an expression which those who were accustomed to the
Greek way of thinking would readily understand.

The letter is addressed to false teachers, including Christians who had fallen into error (2:15). The language of Jude is quoted to denounce these opponents: they are like 'springs without water' (2:17). They promise freedom while they themselves are slaves of depravity. Like 'the dog turning to his own vomit again and the sow that had washed to wallowing in the mire', they had reverted to type. These two scathing quotations, one from Proverbs 26:11 and the other from Greek literature, are skilfully chosen by those who claimed to have inner, esoteric information about the world (2:22).

The lateness of the date of this letter is confirmed by the reference to the letters of Paul as scripture (3:15-16). Ignorant and unreliable teachers had distorted the meaning in some passages of the Pauline epistles which were admittedly hard to understand. How much wiser will be those who follow the recommendations of this letter, if they 'grow in the grace and knowledge of Jesus Christ' whose glory, once shown on the mount, is for ever (2 Pet 3:18).

I JOHN

John writes with a deceptive simplicity. He passes on in an intimate, almost conversational style what he had seen and heard. In this way his evidence, straightforwardly stated, is more convincing than any exhortation (1:1-4).

The atmosphere in which he writes is clearly worldly. In three striking phrases, he analyses what this worldliness is: 'the lust of the flesh, the lust of the eyes, and the pride of life' (2:16). These things have no permanence.

The Christian has 'for ever'. 'Eternal life' is a gift already granted to the believer. It is not only an experience for the future; it can be enjoyed here and now (2:25). There is a promise of the future in it and a taste of the glory that lies ahead.

The importance of distinguishing light from darkness (1:5-2:17) and truth from falsehood (2:18-4:21) arises from the threat of anti-Christs who deny that Jesus is the Christ. There was a subtle error which maintained that Jesus the Christ only appeared to be human. This idea, known as 'Docetism', held that Jesus, the human being, was not essential to the revelation of God. This undermined the Johannine teaching about 'the Word-made-flesh'.

The struggle between light and darkness brings out the point that love is expressed through obedience to God's commandments (5:3). Love overcomes hate and all unrighteousness is sin (5:17).

The conclusion of this letter, which in form is more like a homily, presents a list of certainties 'we know – we know' is repeated many times to counteract the false 'gnostic' knowledge.

Summary

1:1-4	'Life eternal is communion with God'
1:5-2:17	'God is light: he overcomes darkness'
2:18-4:21	'Truth and Falsehood'
5:1-12	'The Victory of Faith'
5:13-21	'We know that the Son of God is come'

Discussion still continues about the authorship of this letter. It is thought by some that it was written by John the elder (see 2 and 3 John), rather than by the author of the fourth gospel. A note-worthy omission in the Revised Standard Version is 1 John 5:7. This verse, with its explicit reference to the Trinity, does not appear in the most reliable manuscripts. It was included in the Vulgate Latin version and its source was a fourth-century Latin text. The authorised version (1611) translated it as follows:

'There are three that bare record in heaven, the Father, the Word, and the holy Ghost: and these three are one.'

II JOHN

It is difficult to accept that this is a personal letter. 'The Elder' who writes to 'the elect Lady' (verse 1) is probably John the elder writing to a local church. It has been suggested that this is a charge written perhaps to the Christian community at Ephesus. Not only is love at the heart of the message, but truth also is of pressing importance (2). The manner of addressing the church in this way is somewhat cryptic, probably on account of the opposition which the faithful were facing. Deceivers and an anti-Christs (7) were threatening. So serious is this hostility that such should not be welcomed into the homes of the Christians (10). 2 John has been regarded as a post-script to 1 John by some scholars.

III JOHN

By way of contrast, the third epistle of John is much more like a letter with its intimate style and personal references. The Elder (or presbyter) may be the title used of a recognised teacher in the church. We are given a glimpse of church life: Gaius (1) has evidently been entrusted with a measure of leadership and responsibility. Diotrephes (9) has been causing trouble; the 'elder' will make a point of mentioning this, when he comes (10). Demetrius has clearly done well and has stood up for the truth.

This letter was not quoted in early Christian writings until the fourth century.

JUDE

This letter, consisting of only 25 verses, contains a warning for the faithful. There is clearly some emergency threatening. The faithful need to remember the mistakes made in the past by those who disobeyed God. Jude writes of the godless who change 'the grace of our God into a licence for immorality' (verse 4). Shades of Sodom and Gomorrah, Cain, Balaam, Korah are painful reminders of the consequences, not only of faithlessness but of rebellion.

Poetry and rhetoric describe with colourfulness the damage these intruders upon Christian community can cause. 'Clouds without rain, blown along by the wind, autumn trees, without fruit and uprooted – twice dead'. Powerful stuff! 'Wild waves of the sea foaming up their shame; wandering stars, for whom blackest darkness has been reserved for ever' (verses 12 and 13).

Scoffers, too, must be guarded against. They deride and try to break up the unity of the Christians and seek to divide people into 'spiritual' or 'carnal'. The duty of the faithful is to build up a body of believers: 'Be merciful to those who doubt; snatch others from the fire and save them' (verses 22 and 23).

The doxology fits the mood. Praise is given to him 'who is able to keep you from falling' (verse 24).

We do not know who Jude was. There are many suggestions: he might have been the Lord's brother. Not often are there references to Genesis. Jude and 2 Peter make similar use of the examples quoted.

THE REVELATION OF ST JOHN THE DIVINE

This book is the only example of apocalyptic writing in the New Testament. There were, however, many Jewish writings in the last two centuries before Christ which were apocalyptic in style and in their spiritual message. Apocalypse means 'revelation'. It has prophetical elements and yet is distinct from prophecy. In the Old Testament, the prophets, hearing the word of the Lord, proclaimed it through preaching and song. At a later stage, prophets such as Ezekiel, Daniel and Zechariah showed themselves as visionaries as well as prophets. As a development of this, those who write 'apocalypses' did not so much preach to people, addressing them face to face, but rather they wrote their visions down in a book.

John (1:9) heard a voice and the voice said 'Write'. Although Justin Martyr in the second century thought that this John was the same writer as the author of the fourth gospel, it is remarkable that the Revelation in many parts of the church was not included in the canon until the fifth century.

Yet it is Johannine. It was probably written in the reign of the Emperor Domitian, a time of terror for the Christians (A.D. 90-95). There is the awareness that the churches are very small, organised in tiny groups as a struggling minority. In spite of the good news that Christ is alive and triumphant, idolatry continues. 'Emperor worship' strikes fear among the faithful and supplies a constant threat. Christians are put in prison and are killed.

The Revelation, for all its poetry and strange imagery, is a very practical piece of writing. It is written to help those who are dismayed. It is written for ordinary people who, unlike ourselves, would have understood much of the symbolism, current in those days. The angels, the trumpets, the seals, and the beasts are all included in the language of apocalypse. John writes not to baffle, but to explain; not to wrap up the present or the future in mystery, but rather to unfold the hidden meaning of all that is happening and to throw light upon it as a result of what he saw on the island of Patmos.

Some of this pastoral purpose of Revelation has come clearer as a result of recent studies of other apocalyptic writings.

There is an atmosphere of catastrophe, yet through the disaster God will intervene and bring in a new age. The details will not be disclosed; the book is sealed. The symbols are weird and un-earthly because 'all things will be made new', and other-worldly.

There is mention of the End at several points in the book (8:1; 10:6-7; 11:15 - 12:1; 15 - 17:1), for the vision of the End fills the whole word picture. There is no historical sequence, no exact chronology. 'After this' is the cue for the next vision.

'Seven' was a symbol in apocalyptic language for 'complete-ness'. Of the 7 churches, the first and last are threatened with ex-tinction; the 2nd and 6th are given unqualified praise; the 3rd, 4th and 5th are both complimented and castigated.

The throne is a symbol of power and authority. God is Emperor. Satanic is the Roman emperor-worship.

Long ago in Babylon and Persia the sun, moon and seven planets had been worshipped as 'seven spirits'.

The book has had great influence on art down through the cen-turies. The picture includes:

1. John's vision of the seven churches (1:1-20)
2. Letters to the seven churches (2:1-3:22)

    Ephesus, courageous but unenthusiastic

    Smyrna, harassed

    Pergamum, too willing to compromise

    Thyatira, over-tolerant

    Sardis – spiritually dead

    Philadelphia – a good report

    Laodicea – complacent
3. Colourful picture of the adoration of the Creator (4:1-11)
4. The sealed book and the Lamb, symbol of self-sacrifice (5:1-14)
5. Opening of the seals; (6:1-17)

    The four horsemen

    War unleashed

    'The wrath of the Lamb'

6.   'Those who washed their robes'; (7:1-17)
       the Christian martyrs

7.   The seventh seal broken (8:1-13)

8.   The demonic forces (9:1-21)

9.   Christ and anti-Christ (10:1-11)

10.   The Law and the Prophets and the New Covenant (11:14-19)

11.   Ascension of Christ – Downfall of Satan (12:1-17)

12.   The Roman Empire – the beast (13-15)

13.   Armageddon (16)
       The downfall of Babylon (Rome) (17-18)

14.   Christ – the fifth Horseman – 'the Word of God' (19:1-20:3)
       The millennium – messianic age (20:4-15)

15.   The heavenly Jerusalem (21 and 22)

Chronological Table

c. 2110	The age of Abraham
c. 1700-1650	The Hebrews in Egypt
c. 1230	The Exodus from Egypt
c. 1085	Samson, judge in Israel
c. 1063	Call of Samuel, judge and prophet (seer)
c. 1025	Saul, King of the Hebrews
c. 1010	Samuel anoints David
c. 1002	Death of Samuel
c. 1000	David, King
985	Nathan, prophet
971	Nathan anoints Solomon
970	Solomon, King
939	Ahijah prophecies division of kingdom

Judah		*Israel*	
931	Rehoboam, King	931	Jeroboam, King
916	Asa, King	841	Jehu, King
870	Jehoshaphat, King	885	Omri, King
781	Uzziah, King	874	Ahab, King
740	Jothan, King	782	Jeroboam II, King
736	Ahaz, King	737	Pekah, King
716	Hezekiah, King	732–724	Hosea, King
642	Amon, King		
609	Jehoahaz, King		
609	Jehoiakim, King		
598	Jehoiachin, King		
598-587	Zedekiah, King		

The Books of the Bible

Genesis (Gen)	Proverbs (Prov)
Exodus (Ex)	Ecclesiastes (Ecc)
Leviticus (Lev)	Song of Songs (Ca)
Numbers (Numb)	Isaiah (Isa)
Deuteronomy (Duet)	Jeremiah (Jer)
Joshua (Jos)	Lamentations (Lam)
Judges (Jg)	Ezekiel (Ezek)
Ruth (Ru)	Daniel (Dan)
1 Samuel (1 Sam)	Hosea (Hos)
2 Samuel (2 Sam)	Joel (Jl)
1 Kings (1 Kgs)	Amos (Am)
2 Kings (2 Kgs)	Obadiah (Ob)
1 Chronicles (1 Chron)	Jonah (Jon)
2 Chronicles (2 Chron)	Micah (Mic)
Ezra (Ezr)	Nahum (Nah)
Nehemiah (Neh)	Habakkuk (Hab)
Esther (Est)	Zephaniah (Zeph)
Job (Job)	Haggai (Hag)
Psalms (Ps)	Zechariah (Zech)
	Malachi (Mal)

Apocrypha (Apoc)

1 Esdras (1 Esd)

2 Esdras (2 Esd)

Tobit (Tob)

Judith (Jdt)

Additions to Esther (Ad Est)

Wisdom (Wis)

Ecclesiasticus (Ecclus)

Baruch (Bar)

Song of 3 Children (S 3 Ch)

Susanna (Sus)

Bel and the Dragon (Bel)

Prayer of Manasseh (Man)

1 Maccabees (1 Mac)

2 Maccabees (2 Mac)

New Testament (NT)

Matthew (Mt)

Mark (Mk)

Luke (Lk)

John (Jn)

Acts (Ac)

Romans (Rom)

1 Corinthians (1 Cor)

2 Corinthians (2 Cor)

Galatians (Gal)

Ephesians (Eph)

Philippians (Phil)

Colossians (Col)

1 Thessalonians (1 Th)

2 Thessalonians (2 Th)

1 Timothy (1 Tim)

2 Timothy (2 Tim)

Titus (Tit)

Philemon (Phm)

Hebrews (Heb)

James (Jas)

1 Peter (1 Pet)

2 Peter (2 Pet)

1 John (1 Jn)

2 John (2 Jn)

3 John (3 Jn)

Jude (Jude)

Revelations (Rev)